MW00979084

CYBER WARRIOR

The Ultimate Manifesto

For Internet Usage

and Profiteering

by Luree

UPHILL PUBLISHING LTD.

Published in 1998 by Uphill Publishing Ltd.
180 Attwell Drive, Suite 400, Toronto, Canada M9W 6A9

First printing: September 1998

Luree
Cyber warrior: the ultimate manifesto
for internet usage and profiteering

Includes index.
ISBN 1-896912-10-9

1. Internet (Computer network). I. Title.

ZA4201.L87 1998   025.04   C98-931442-1

Editor: Uphill Publishing Ltd.
Cover Artwork: Twister Graphics
Printed in Canada

Dedicated to my terrific brother, Bryan,
whom I'll always look up to.

Thank you for your help and encouragement.

Table of Contents

THE REQUISITE DISCLAIMER

Chapter One

Introducing the Cyber Warrior

■ ■ ■ ■ ■ ■ ■

You've got a computer. You've got a modem. You've got a connection to the Internet. You have a desire to make some money. Now what?

- This is a book of ideas and answers.

- It's not for computer professionals.

- It's not for cyber geniuses.

- It's for the average person who would like to make their on-line time pay for itself and more.

- It's for the person who doesn't want to become a full-time geek, nerd or wizard.

- It's for someone who wants to use the Internet to seek new opportunities and fearlessly chart new territory.

- It's for progressive thinkers who dare to be rebels.

- It's for the secret Cyber Warriors in our midst

- It's for *you!*

> **Warrior Byte**
>
> Not too sure of your net surfing skills? Don't despair—get yourself over to:
>
> **http://www.learnthenet.com/**

FINDING YOUR WAY

As long as you know how to read and click a mouse, you'll be able to find the information you need. Scattered throughout the pages of this book are little boxes that contain **Warrior Bytes.** These morsels of information give you concise directions to appropriate websites that pertain to a particular topic of discussion. You will also see little boxes containing **Warrior Weapons.** These will remind you that some of the material you will encounter has been discussed in previous chapters. They will help you remember terms that may be unfamiliar to you.

Armed with the computer Jump Disk at the back of this book, you can go directly to the destinations mentioned in the Warrior Bytes. To take advantage of this feature, insert the disk into the A: drive of your computer. Connect to the Internet. Open up your web browser of choice. *Netscape* or *Internet Explorer* are recommended but not necessary. In your browser go to the FILE menu, in the upper left corner of your screen. Choose OPEN FILE and then choose **A:\start.htm**. You'll be able to thoroughly explore the Internet destinations mentioned in this book.

The **start.htm** page corresponds with the index in the book. To access the specific chapter and section you want, click on the bullets or bullet holes to the left of the subtitles. You can stop the sounds and animation by clicking on the STOP button at the top of your web browser. For super-speedy web surfing, disable the images so that you only see the printed information on our screen. This way you'll be spending less time waiting for all those fancy graphics to download.

To disable images in Netscape, open the OPTIONS menu on the top of the screen. Remove the check mark to the left of AUTO LOAD IMAGES and you will no longer download any pictures while surfing. The check mark disappears when you click on this option and reappears when you click it again.

In *Microsoft Internet Explorer* you can disable images by choosing OPTIONS in the EDIT menu at the top of the screen. Click on GENERAL and then look at the choices under MULTIMEDIA. By clicking on the SHOW PICTURES field, you will remove the little check mark. To learn more about how your web browser works, use the HELP button or read one of the many books available on the subject.

The advantage of disabling AUTO LOAD IMAGES is that it speeds things up. Experienced surfers use this nifty trick so that they don't have to wait for all those big, fancy animated graphics and photographs to load onto their computer. If you're looking for plain, no-frills information and are short on time, get rid of the images and your pages will load a lot faster.

Another way to speed things up is to disable JAVA, which is a specialized computer language. Go to NETWORK PREFERENCES, then to LANGUAGES. Remove the checks on JAVA and JAVA SCRIPT.

You've probably heard *herds* of acronyms, like DOS, SCSI, WYSIWYG, etc. Well PCMCIA! (People Can't Memorize Computer Industry Acronyms). Don't worry if you can't remember what all those crazy initials mean. You don't have to speak geek to be a Cyber Warrior…and don't be afraid to try those different buttons on your Internet browser. It's highly unlikely that you'll do any damage. If things don't work out, just shut off your computer and reboot. You'll be starting with a fresh screen again.

There's a lot of information packed between these covers. The best advice is to go at your own speed. Look at the various websites as you read through the chapters. You'll find that your mind will start percolating when confronted with the overwhelming mass of business ideas. Keep a notepad beside you and jot down your own moneymaking ideas as you surf. You've got the warrior instinct already! This book and Jump Disk will help you zero in on the opportunities you can use.

Warrior Byte

URL,GIF,PCMIA,MPEG,MIME, etc. It's all *Geek* to me! You're not the only one who wonders what all those strange acronyms mean. You need a good translator at:

http://www.netlingo.com/

> **Warrior Byte**
>
> If that's not enough to satisfy your curiosity, there's more at:
>
> **http://www.netdictionary.com/html/wordlist. html**
>
> N.B. These sites provide a complete glossary of computer and Internet terms. This is an invaluable learning tool—
>
> USE IT!

WHY YOU NEED TO BE A CYBER WARRIOR

- You're bored or retired, with time on your hands. You might as well use that time to make money, right?

- You're scrambling to make ends meet and you need some ideas to make extra money.

- You realize that knowledge is vital to your development and ignorance is anathema. You instinctively crave the new technology that can provide unique income opportunities.

- You know that the business world is a combat zone and you don't want to enter it unarmed.

- You're just plain curious about nabbing all that secret information that's on the World Wide Web.

- You're ticked off at seeing your taxes going into the pockets of unproductive civil servants.

- You're disturbed by the government waste that eats up everything you've worked so hard to attain. You've seen evidence of political corruption, but feel powerless to stop it and you want to know how you can keep the money you make.

Cyber Warriors are stealthy and smart. They know how to use the Internet to get what they want. In the modern world, where knowledge is king, their services will be in great demand and they will be respected members of the Internet Business Community.

This book is designed to get you started quickly, easily and as painlessly as possible and the information provided herein is for entertainment purposes only. Where you take this knowledge is entirely up to you, but the author does not advocate that you do anything illegal in your country or elsewhere!

WHY YOU NEED THE INTERNET

"Without information, a really clever person cannot get started. With information, a much less clever person can get very far."

-Edward de Bono (English writer)

Warrior Byte

If you would like to sound more intelligent by quoting someone else, just visit:

Famous and Not So Famous Quotations at:

**http://www.labyrinth.net.au/~pirovich/
quotes.html**

or *Good Quotations by Famous People* at:

http://www.cs.virginia.edu/~robins/quotes.html

Try doing your own Internet search for *quotable quotes* or *famous quotations...* and don't forget the wonderful wisdom of *Emo Phillips* at:

**http://www.nd.edu/~emerkler/emo/
quotes.html**

WHAT THE INTERNET CAN DO FOR YOU

If you've had doubts about getting an Internet connection, you haven't considered what the Internet can do for you:

- It helps you develop new skills and interests. When you're wired (connected to the Internet), you can't help but learn something about the new technology and its applications.

- It promotes self-confidence because you become your own teacher. Learn what you need to know at your own pace, without fear or criticism. With the Internet, you do things by yourself, for yourself... you are self-propelled and self-contained.

- It increases your chances of making a better income. With only 12% of the world connected to the Internet, you will be one of the elite—one of the minority who has access to unlimited knowledge. You'll be on the ground floor of opportunity.

- It broadens your horizons—You can find romance, share ideas, interact with people of different cultures and civilizations.

- It provides a tremendous opportunity to network in your business and to expand your contact base worldwide.

- It helps you become a better person by opening your mind to new ideas, political information, medical research and so much more! As you become more informed, you can utilize your new-found knowledge to help those close to you. Knowledge breeds respect. Your thoughts and decisions will be taken more seriously because you will have the facts to give them substance.

The Internet has already spurred a revolution. It has revolutionized the way we communicate, play, do business, gather information and share knowledge. The world will never be the same. Whether you apply what you will learn in this book or not, you will be still be at an advantage over those who are not connected to the Net. Getting "wired" is not expensive—even a second-hand computer with a 14400 modem will allow you access.

Once you're wired, you'll have at your disposal one of the most rapid and cost-effective methods ever developed to communicate with people worldwide. Faster than your local post office and cheaper than a long distance phone call, E-mail is the warrior's ultimate method of communication. Simply by choosing this most economical and convenient method, you side-step the dominance of government monopolies and big business conglomerates.

You are tapping into one of the greatest knowledge resources that has ever been available to mankind. Just think about the effect that will have on human progress. There will be no excuse for ignorance because the truth—and the facts—are readily available.

You have immediate access to professional advice regarding your personal problems. No matter what situation you are facing—medical or financial problems, grief therapy, alcoholism, loneliness, natural or mechanical issues and more, there is bound to be someone among the thirty million or so Internet users who can help. Usenet newsgroups, chat groups, mailing lists and web pages are all resources that are easy and convenient to use... and now lie at your fingertips.

You have a wonderful opportunity to promote your business. No matter what you're selling, you'll be able to convey information to potential customers through your web page. You'll be able to answer questions and make constant contact with clients through E-mail. The Internet is quickly becoming a vital component in any successful business venture.

The Internet is rapidly and continuously expanding, like an exploding supernova. Its unprecedented growth exceeds millions of new subscribers annually, providing ongoing opportunities to meet new people, share ideas, explore new products and conduct worldwide business on a scale so far-reaching, no one could have imagined.

You have a chance to publish information that is important to you. Through web pages and newsgroups, you can exercise your democratic right to freedom of speech. You may not agree with what appears on the Net and others may disagree with what you publish, but you are asserting one of the most important rights character-istic of a true democratic system.

You have the opportunity to participate in one of the greatest potential instruments for world peace that has ever been developed. Whether you are confined to a wheelchair or are tremendously active and athletic, your thoughts are equally valuable. Through open discussion, various races, religions and political persuasions can openly express their philosophies and settle their differ-ences in the most civilized way possible. How absolute-ly wonderful for mankind!

Don't miss out on any of the fun and all of the benefits that the World Wide Web offers. Isn't it time you got wired?

THE IMPACT OF THE INTERNET

The Internet is still a novelty in most people's lives. Just recently, the average citizen has begun to realize that the Internet is the world's biggest encyclopedia. Now, more and more people who crave enlightenment are getting wired. What great potential for human advancement! Scientists and medical researchers can share new discoveries and ideas at lightning speed—with miraculous results. Technology is advancing by quantum leaps, due to the synergy that results from this advanced level of communication. People are sharing with and learning from those of different cultures, faiths and ideals, resulting in an opportunity to replace prejudice and ignorance with understanding and tolerance. What a great time to be alive!

Don't be deceived, though, with this open communication. The underbelly of humanity is also exposed. Sexism, racism, pornography, and a myriad of other ills abound on the Internet. They also reflect our society, but the Internet gives us a fighting chance to confront these ideas and dismiss them as ridiculous. The Internet is truly a tool of democracy—*exercise your vote* by not visiting websites that you find offensive. Share your opinions and values with others, but do so carefully and with discretion. Remember: nothing is hidden—everything is out in the open on the Internet.

If you were naive prior to your introduction to the Net, you won't be for long. You will discover that most governments are corrupt, for example. This sad fact is readily observable in our own democracies, which don't allow citizens to spend their money where they want or on what they want. (If you don't believe this is true, consider how much money you are allowed to take out of your country without declaring it). Consider what products are subject to high trade tariffs or banned altogether from entering your country. Furthermore, those with power want to keep it. By restricting access to information, leaders are able to keep their people ignorant and under control. Information is power.

Recall the Dark Ages (no, not in your personal life). Religious leaders certainly didn't want their followers asking any questions. Everything had to be accepted with blind faith. All thoughts had to be approved by the clergy. Of course, this set scientific inquiry back hundreds of years. Many people were killed, tortured and imprisoned for questioning truths that we take for granted today. We'd still believe that the sun revolved around the earth, if left to the fundamentalists. Thank goodness for man's inquiring mind. (God only knows what misinformed "truths" we still cling to).

Repressive regimes are running scared. They know that it is possible to keep their women, children and citizens under control through fear (fear that is perpetuated through lack of knowledge), but they'll never gain the respect of the global community once they are exposed. Dictators have to go to sleep at night with the thought that there are a lot of unhappy people who wish their leader were dead. In every country governed by oppressive laws, there is always an underground to circumvent them. Now we have the World Wide Web to expose them.

The most dangerous threat to our freedom is the fact that governments can control our Internet Service Providers. Eventually, everybody will want to be connected to the Internet, just like everybody now has television access. It will become a way of life for a large part of the world's population. The way to make computers obtainable is to lower their price and the most effective way to do so is to strip the guts out of them and connect them to one big provider that does all the computing.

If you believe that the government elite won't use this to control the content of those who use the Internet through a government network, then you haven't been paying attention. Newspapers everywhere are talking about collective computing technology that will be controlled by those in power—and content will be determined by their whims of censorship. You may personally believe in censorship, but what if your own ideas and beliefs are being censored? Definitely a possibility if you are a member of a minority religion or an environmentalist, for example.

Once censorship starts, there is no stopping it. It merely becomes a matter of degree. You may think there are certain things that your children aren't ready to view and there are plenty of software products available to help you limit a child's surfing to family-approved sites. However, you won't ever be able to curb their curiosity. It's highly unlikely you'll be able to stop them from visiting a friend, a data café, a library or any other location that has free access to the Internet.

The best protection you can give your children is your own guidance. Just as the Internet allows people to freely exchange ideas, you have the opportunity to freely exchange ideas with your children. If pornography upsets you, talk to your children openly about your views on the subject and ask them how they would feel if their mother or sisters were involved. Ask them if they think people can be forced, through economic circumstances or otherwise, to perform in unnatural ways.

Consider visiting controversial sites with your children so that they can see the other side of the business— the side where children get hurt and killed and women used like commodities. As much as it may disturb you to expose your children to this information, you will be doing them a favor in the long run by opening them up to informed discussion without fear of censorship. You will be giving them the opportunity to form values that will stay with them because they agree with what you are saying, rather than being forced to adopt what you say.

> **Warrior Byte**
>
> Are you worried about child safety on the Information Highway? Put it into perspective:
>
> **http: //www.larrysworld.com/child_safety.html**

It's the hidden truths that pose the most danger to our children. How many teenagers are afraid to admit they have sex and, as a consequence, don't take proper precautions to prevent disease or pregnancy? How many girls are afraid to admit they are pregnant and end up dying at the hands of back street abortionists? You are never going to *control* your children by just saying "no". Try uncensored discussion with them. Openly share your ideas and your reasoning and be prepared to listen to theirs. They'll be much more receptive. You won't gain their respect by being a tyrant and you'll find it's virtually impossible to "walk through a closed door" (i.e. force your own ideas on them).

What is true for your family should be true for the Internet. Be aware and wary of government leaders who want to try and control the Internet. What they really want to do is control your thoughts. Watch out for the censor monster. When you don't have access to the information on both sides of an issue, you are in danger of being controlled by one side only (not necessarily the side that has your best interest in mind). Use every opportunity to tell people the good things that are happening because of the Internet. Rise up against every bill that would restrict your freedom.

Cyber Warrior

With all of the above in mind, use your democratic right to go out and make money. This book contains some powerful information. It represents many hours of research, but it also explains how you can do your own research. You don't have to be a cyber-genius to find out what you need to know and then apply it. You just have to be willing to fight for the right to freedom of information.

Warrior Byte

Get connected! A list of active service providers all over the world:

http://thelist.internet.com/

Get somewhere! *Super Search* for a unique way of finding what you want:

http://www.webscout.com/search/search.html

Get going! An archive of selected sites that provides a reference point for browsing the web:

http://www.bigeye.com

You don't need to spend money to get a lot of the information that's on the Internet. *Freenets* are, in most cases, manned by volunteers and operated by donations. Help is provided and many may be accessed from your local library. Here's a list of Freenets around the world, plus information on how to use them:

http://www.fcl.metronet.lib.mi.us/MIKEL/fm /index.html

Chapter Two

ANALYZING YOURSELF

■ ■ ■ ■ ■ ■ ■

Why do you want to be involved with the new technology? Weren't you perfectly happy with your old way of doing things? If you answered "I want to make more money", remember that money itself is just paper. The reality is, the making of money is not the central issue; generating it through some activity that aligns with your true self, is what will truly satisfy you. *"Do what you love and the money will follow..."*

There are lots of ways to make money. It can be generated legally, illegally, or somewhere in between. Money can come from risky ventures (which keep your stomach in knots and the adrenaline pumping) or it can be generated through small, secure investments. Never doubt that there's money to be made. The question is "How do *you* want to make it?".

WHAT DO YOU WANT AND HOW BADLY DO YOU WANT IT?

There are a number of books on the market that teach you computer programming, web page design, marketing, and financial and business management. This book will guide you to the gold—huge, untapped caverns of it—yours for the taking. Use this book as your map to the mother lode. It'll show you where to dig. Your own talents and intelligence will be all the tools you'll need to mine the opportunities.

Like any good warrior, you must depend on yourself—on your inner and outer strength. You have to do the work, learn the new skills and technology, promote yourself and be prepared for the consequences that result from applying this knowledge.

You are unique and so is every web page on the Internet. There may be a thousand people out there doing the same thing you do, but there is only one person doing it your way. Find your niche on the Internet. Do it different from anyone else and do it better.

Warrior Byte

"Human energy cannot be made to work efficiently except in an atmosphere of individual freedom and voluntary cooperation, based on enlightened self interest and moral responsibility."

- Henry Grady Weaver, The Mainspring of Human Progress

Another valuable website is The Foundation for Economic Education:

http://www.self-gov.org/freeman/

THE WARRIOR MENTALITY

If you intend to go exploring in the cyber jungle, you'd better know yourself intimately. You'll be facing uncharted territory armed only with the most rudimentary knowledge. You'll encounter vermin ready to crawl all over the innocent and unsuspecting. Beware, for example, the government monster who would like nothing more than to drain the lifeblood from your business and feast on its entrails. Roaming the cyber jungle are leeches and scum-suckers, slithering snakes and sneaky little rodents.

Then again, there are many wonderful, sincere, helpful people who make up the cyber community. Fortunately, the good guys far outnumber the bad. Who are you? You will be relating to people on a non-physical level and dealing with pure ideas. You'll be depending on your own capacity for communication. No one else knows who's inside you (saint or savage) until you hit the keyboard.

> How do you begin? With yourself! Before experimenting with any of the information in this book, you should measure your own tolerance for risk.

> How uncomfortable are you taking a risk? Do you derive a great deal of satisfaction from reaching goals you've set for yourself? How far are you willing to go?

> What is your deeper desire—respect or money? Perhaps you can have both. Maybe not.

Are you concerned about immoral activity? How low will you stoop?

Are you prepared to rebel against those laws that you feel are unfair?

Are you happy with your life? Are you prepared to risk losing your friends, family and assets in the pursuit of money?

Do you really want to hurt anyone? Unethical business practices can result in financial ruin, emotional burnout and destruction of personal relationships. Unqualified advice can cause psychological harm and physical danger.

Are you prepared to follow through with a business plan once you've developed one?

Evaluate your motives! Some of these questions may set off a personal alarm—take a close and honest look at what motivates you and weigh that against any possible gain or loss you may incur. Never do something that compromises your personal values. Be true to yourself. If you feel, for example, that sexual exploitation is wrong, steer away from trying to generate income through cyber-porn. Keep your conscience clear at all times. If you feel that the laws of our country are ludicrous, utilize the Internet to examine and evaluate them and share your opinion with others—gain strength in numbers and use that clout to change the laws. Remember: You have to respect yourself in the morning.

Warrior Byte

What kind of credit report is out on you? Find out at:

http://www.creditbureau.com/reports.html

For a general snooping, you can find out more about someone entering their E-mail address in the *FINGER* client located on this page. If you want to find out which country an Internet Service Provider originates from, just type it in here. Lots of preliminary information on people and ISPs is available using the connection on this website:

http://www.cd.chalmers.se/~peterk/wois.htm

WEB PAGES

Warrior Byte

You have a right to privacy and security. Here's how to surf safely in cyber space:

**http://infoweb.magi.com/~privcan/pubs/
cber.html**

Surfing the Net is similar to leafing through a giant magazine. It contains advertising, information and amusement. Each page offers something different for you to explore. The Internet contains a universe of fun and learning for Cyber Warriors. Go fearlessly—brave new territory—grow and learn at your own pace.

There are basically two kinds of websites on the Internet. Those that appeal to the intellect and those that appeal to the viscera. People are on the Internet either to learn something or to be entertained. Examples of intellectually stimulating sites are those that tell you how to avoid taxes, where to get the latest medical help, how to find your genealogy and where to source countless gadgets to help you overcome some of life's hurdles. Entertainment sites let you play games, catch up on gossip, find new friends and so much more. Money-making opportunities abound in both arenas.

Warrior Byte

You can find out if a cyber friend has a home page on the World Wide Web from the E-mail address:

superman@gothamcity.org

You can determine the name of your friend's Internet Service Provider (or ISP). If you type:

http://www.gothamcity.org

in your net browser's location field and hit ENTER, you will arrive at the main page of that provider.

Warrior Byte

Most individual homepages are indexed at the person's Internet name and preceded by a little sign called a *tilde*. The '~' sign is found in the upper left corner of your keyboard. To get to the index page of your Internet friend "superman" you would type:

http://www.gothamcity.org/~superman

If your friend has a home page, the index should show up when you hit the ENTER key. If you get an Error Message like "404 URL not found", this could mean that your friend hasn't put up an Internet page. Of course, you could always send your pal "superman" E-mail asking for his home page address.

In addition, you can get a good idea of the country of origin for any E-mail you receive. Look for a country zone code. For example, .CA is Canada and .AU is Australia. To find out the country zone codes, go to your browser and type:

http://www.newtoo.com/codes.html

in the location field. Also try doing a search for *country zone codes* to find other places on the web that carry this information.

PROMOTE YOURSELF

Use the Internet as a tool to advertise what you do. Let the world know you're there and that you're looking to do business with it. Some promotional methods include:

SIGNATURES

Part of the fun of being a cyber warrior is that you can tell people a little bit about yourself by making up your own unique signature. A signature is a short, witty, often humorous little statement that reflects your personality or advertises your business. Signatures should appear at the end of every E-mail message you write or every newsgroup posting you make. They usually provide some insight into the character of the person sending them.

1. Keep it simple with something like: "Visit my home page. It's Real Kewl! Let me design one like if for you."
   http://www.whoopee.net/~itsme

2. Make it profound with something like: "*'640k should be enough for anybody.'* Bill Gates, 1981 Talk to me about investing in my company."
   http://www.megabucks.com

Use different signatures for different replies. It's fun…so go ahead and create one for yourself. Signatures should be brief (four lines or less) or they become annoying because they take up so much news space.

NEWSGROUPS

Once you've created a few personality-revealing signatures, you'll need to decide which of the twenty thousand plus newsgroups they'll be inflicted on. Learn how to use a news reader program. Participate in newsgroups that relate to your particular field and develop a reputation for friendliness and helpfulness. Build goodwill and sales will follow.

PUBLISH

Create your own web page, newsletter or magazine to promote your business.

ADVERTISE

Consider joining an Internet Mall, where customers shop for many different products at the same site. Promote your web page by listing it with every possible search engine on the Internet.

BE PROFESSIONAL

Conduct your Internet business in the same manner that you would if you were dealing with your customers face-to-face. People respect honesty and integrity, so be sure to cultivate these qualities.

AVOID BEING ANNOYING

Don't send unsolicited E-mail advertising. Many service providers will shut down your account if you SPAM. SPAMMING is the term used for sending out massive volumes of unsolicited E-mail to every address you can find on the Internet. (It's cyberspeak for "junk mail"). Some Internet users have to pay a fee for downloading E-mail. Unwanted mail increases the cost of their Internet access and, consequently, makes them very angry. Sending out millions of E-mails is a cheap form of advertising. If you are determined to conduct business this way and can live with yourself, knowing you'll make a number of E-mail recipients very angry, at least engage the services of a server that allows you to SPAM. Don't let anyone know your real name and E-mail address, or you will be the recipient of many flames. If you don't know what a flame is now, you'll certainly know when you receive one. Flames are E-mails that contain obnoxious, foul and sometimes threatening commentary, usually related to the level of your intelligence.

Warrior Byte

Make sure everyone knows that you're on the Net. Submit your site to over 50 major search engines, directories and Usenet newsgroups!

http://users.boone.net/yinon/multisub/default .html

THE BIG GUN

Warrior Byte

You are entitled to information under the *Freedom of Information Act*. Here's how to file a request:

http://www.well.com/user/fap/foia.htm

Information is the path to knowledge and knowledge is the path to fortune. You can never be too smart and you can never know all there is to know about anything...but you can know more than lots of other people. Sell your knowledge to those who want it.

Knowledge is the most valuable resource you can possess in today's fast-moving world. If you have access to it, just think of the many ways you can put it to good use, helping your family and yourself in the process. You don't need horsepower or muscle power to compete today—you need brain power.

Are you a doodler, a dawdler or a doer? You won't get anything done by reading a book. Get out there and learn your craft hands-on! Join an Internet guild and get your nose into a newsgroup. Ask questions. Keep current—the Net changes daily. Change with it and you'll be ahead of the crowd.

This book doesn't advocate any illegal activity. It will only show you how money can be made and where to get the information to make it. If you find any chapter in this book offensive, don't read it! If you own the book, feel free to tear out the pages that upset you. You are a mature adult with the power to control what you read. You don't have the power to control what other people say or think, but if you're reading this book you're obviously living in a country that allows you the privilege of reading controversial material. Absorb the information that suits you and that you can utilize most effectively and ignore the rest.

All information has the potential to be used for good or evil. As an adult, you are capable of making informed choices once you've digested the appropriate information. Be on the lookout for scams and information overload. Just because you see something in print doesn't mean it's true, accurate or credible. Constantly ask questions. "Is this information accurate and correct? Can I go to the source? Does it have applications I can use?" and ultimately, *"How can I use this information to make money?"*

This book was written to satisfy the craving of the hard-core warrior. What you do with these ideas is up to you. Arm yourself with knowledge! Challenge life! Seek opportunities! Be fearless and confident! Get out there and chart new territory! *Carpe Diem!*

Warrior Byte

What's the Internet all about? Here's the place for both newbies and webmasters:

http://www.webreference.com

CHAPTER THREE

SEARCHING FOR ANSWERS

■ ■ ■ ■ ■ ■ ■

> **Warrior Weapon**
>
> Remember that there is a glossary of all Internet terms right on the Internet.
>
> (See Warrior Byte on page 4)

arriors must be armed and information is the best armament for the modern world. Read any newspaper and you'll discover that the most feared people in any political system are not necessarily those with big guns.

The people imprisoned in the Soviet Union were the intellectuals—the true warriors. The bureaucracy feared them because they were armed with knowledge that could challenge the status quo. Free-thinkers, who understood democracy, were a threat to the ruling class.

Who did China fear most? Unarmed students! They were silenced immediately before their weapon of choice, *democratic knowledge*, could be disseminated among the masses.

Why do fundamentalists of every religion try to deny Internet access to their people? They don't want their followers to start asking questions or thinking for themselves. As long as people believe everything they are told, leaders are safe.

If you want to control a population, keep them ignorant. If you want to control a particular segment of a population, like women or racial minorities, keep them pregnant and struggling to make a living. They won't have time to find out about birth control or how to learn to support themselves. If you ever doubt that knowledge is power, watch the evening news.

Warrior Byte

What countries are allowed Internet access? Check it out:

http://rein.utexas.edu/reenic/Subjects/Comm/ ip.html

THE QUEST FOR KNOWLEDGE

Warrior Byte

Learn how to use the Usenet Newsgroups:

http://sunsite.unc.edu/usent-i/

Learn more about navigating the Internet. Tutorials are available:

http://alabanza.com/kabacoff/Inter-Links/

You are probably constantly asking yourself questions. Even as you read this book, you are having a little conversation in your head. "How can I possibly get any information off that vast Internet? How can I motivate myself to follow through on any of this? How can I make enough money to cover the cost of purchasing this book?" Your mind is constantly questioning. If you search for information, you're bound to find answers.

Before your brain explodes from information overload, you'd better confine yourself to seeking one answer at a time. You can keep your head clear and keep your focus by knowing exactly what you're looking for.

If your primary goal is to make money, you do an Internet search for money. Wow! There must be twenty million documents out there with the word "money" in them! Already you've reached critical mass!

First things first. Write down exactly what you plan to search for, including a few related topics. In your quest for bucks, for example, consider making an idea list like this:

- money
- make money fast
- how to become a millionaire
- income opportunities
- how to accumulate wealth
- how to get rich
- financial advice

Do an Internet search on any one of these topics and you'll gather a mountain of information. By now you probably realize that searching for "money" is much too broad a topic. Remember: You can't eat the whole elephant at once!

SEARCHER BEWARE

While you're searching cyberspace for money, there are lots of people searching for ways to separate you from your money. One of the biggest scams you'll come across is the *Unsecured Offshore Credit Card.* This is a great scam to pull on those new to the Internet. It goes like this:

You receive E-mail or stumble across a website that offers a credit card based at some offshore bank. All you have to do is forward them a money order for $100. They offer you an instant line of credit for $5,000 at this bank, no credit check, no questions asked.

Of course you could use $5,000 worth of credit, so you send in your $100 money order.

You wait...and you wait...and you wait. Finally, you discern that no legitimate bank, onshore or offshore, will give out $5,000 in unsecured credit. In fact, offshore banks require that you have funds in an account from which they can deduct any credit purchases made.

It's not worth going to small claims court to try and recoup your $100 from someone who lives thousands of miles away. You've just paid your tuition to the *School of Hard Knocks*.

Another money scam that often plagues the Internet is the *Offshore Investment Company*. Here the operators advertise for investors in their offshore company. They offer extremely high, tax-free rates of return that sound too good to be true. They are. Once these offshore companies have your money, they mysteriously disappear.

Warrior Byte

There are many scams lurking for the unwary surfer. MLMs (Multi-Level Marketing) and telephone scams abound. Never respond to a phone number in an unsolicited E-mail ad. Be especially wary of 809 or 649 prefix numbers. Many of these scammers make money when you rack up a huge long-distance bill while waiting on hold. If you are unsure about something that sounds too good to be true, surf over to *Scambusters*:

http://www.scambustersorg/scamlinks.html

Perhaps you'd have more luck searching for specific kinds of money. Refine your search to look for *government grants, business loans, venture capital* and *finder's fees.* You will no longer be limiting your search to money, but will be sourcing money that is available to people just like you. Tweak your search further by tapping into "sources of government money available for starting business". When you plug in a big, long search field, you'll get a concise, relevant list of returns. By searching through these, you'll come up with ways to shorten your field to encompass very exact information. This takes a bit of practice and, like any skill, practice takes time.

Warrior Byte

Use the Mother of all search engines. If the type of search engine you need isn't here, then it may not exist:

http://www.thecodex.com/search.html

Knowledge is gold. You're going to have to learn how to pan for nuggets of information on the Net and then, like an alchemist, turn them into money. Innovative and resourceful people (just like you) are making good money selling what they know. It's up to you to gain a thorough knowledge of a particular subject and prosper from it. It's all there on the Net, at your fingertips. Just reach for it. The whole world is your library. Converse with experts, in virtually any field of endeavor, through E-mail, a chat room and newsgroups.

> **Warrior Byte**
>
> This book assumes that you have some familiarity with E-mail, chat, telnet and newsgroups. These are the Cyber Warrior's weapons. Here are some sources for good programs in each of these areas. These websites are also helpful:
>
> E-mail:
>
> *Eudora* **http://www.eudora.com**
>
> Newsgroups:
>
> *Free Agent* **http://www.forteinc.com/forte/**
>
> Chat:
>
> *mIRC* **http://www.mirc.co.uk/**
>
> Telnet:
>
> *anzio lite* **http://www.ansiocom/anziolite.html**

SEARCH ENGINES

There are hundreds of different search engines scattered throughout the Internet. Each search engine works a little differently. To become an aggressive searcher, you'll need to become familiar with the inner workings of a few of your favorites.

Read the Help! The three most important words you'll ever hear (at least where the Internet is concerned) are "Read the Help". Every search engine on the Internet comes with a help section. *No one ever reads it!*

Many people seem to have a genetic predisposition to ignoring instructions and will *never* ask directions! No wonder everyone is trying to find themselves these days! The bottom line is, you'll cut your learning curve drastically by checking out the help section...and make it easy on yourself.

Warrior Byte

To find lots of different search engines, just type the word *search* in your browser's location field. Hit the ENTER key and you'll be at a great search site.

Search everywhere! This site has everything for quick and easy searches:

http://www.cobleskill.edu/webtools/search.htm

Here's a search engine for everything in the world:

http://www.hamrad.com/search.html

Do you need the power of ten different search engines at once? This site includes searches of FTP and Usenet. Head for the *Dog Pile*:

http://www.dogpile.com

If your favorite search engine is too busy, scoot over to this one:

http://www.cronet.com/~mprofaca/search4.html

It's amazing how much information is out there. Each link not only takes you to a new web page, it can connect you to a whole different country, so you can tour the world right from your desktop!

If you are using Internet Explorer as your browser, quickly search for a specific subject by typing *go(subject)* or *?(subject)* in the location field at the top of the screen (sometimes called the address bar). To find the finest earthworms, type *?earthworms.* This will connect you with Yahoo's search engine immediately. Yahoo is a website that specializes in organizing all the different World Wide Web sites.

Here's a quick PC tip if you hate typing. If someone sends you a lengthy Internet address in a document or E-mail, just drag your mouse across it so it's highlighted in black. Press your RIGHT mouse button and a little edit menu will pop up. Click on COPY. Now go over to your Internet browser and place your cursor in the location field. (The cursor is that flashing little black bar and the location field is the white space at the top of your browser where you can type in the Internet addresses). Click your RIGHT mouse button and choose PASTE. The Internet address should now appear in the location field. All you have to do is hit the ENTER button and you'll be going to your destination somewhere in cyberspace.

One of the cool things about the Netscape browser is that you don't have to type some humongous Internet address in order to get somewhere. Netscape will add that annoying **http://** (hypertext transfer protocol) as well as the **www.** (World Wide Web) and the **.com** (commercial network). That makes life a whole lot easier! For any commercial (.com) Internet address, just type the main word. Netscape will fill in the rest when you hit the ENTER key. Most major businesses have their own domain name. A domain name is one that has been registered so that no one else can use it. For example: to find the Ford Motor Company, try typing the word *ford* in the location field. Hit the ENTER key. Now you're surfin'!

Warrior Byte

Use the Mother of all search engines. If the type of search engine you need isn't here, then it may not exist:

http://www.thecodex.com/search.html

THE BASICS

Warrior Byte

The *Internet Public Library* is a good starting point for serious research at:

http://ipl.sils.umich.edu

The *Virtual Reference Collection* contains information on jobs, grants, zip codes, encyclopedia and many vital topics. Definitely worth a visit at:

http://www.lib.uc.edu/home/virtual.html

Way back in the 19th century, lived a mathematician named George Boole. He developed an operations system based on symbols for common words such as *and, or, not, with* and *near.* These *Boolean Operators* are what make most search engines run. Learn to use them.

Let's say you want to bake some scrumptious homemade doggie goodies for Fido and want to find a stimulating new recipe on the Internet. It's important that you give the search engine the correct information in order to find what you need. If you ask for "dog biscuits", you could end up with a thousand web pages from companies that sell canine cookies. If you want to bake your own treats, be sure to ask for "dog biscuit recipes" and Make sure your spelling is correct! Use capital letters where appropriate, particularly with names of persons. Give it a try. Pick out any search engine and type in a request. Click on the SEARCH button. Something is bound to come back.

At this point you probably have a screenful of Links to various web pages on the Internet that contain information about the topic of your search. If you haven't found what you're looking for, try rephrasing the question or selecting a different search engine. This is one of the simplest ways to get information from the World Wide Web, but you can refine your search for more specific information. Sourcing information from the giant library that is the Internet is one of the most useful skills you can learn.

Warrior Byte

Tap into the most current directory of information on-line:

**http://whowhereconnectnow.whowhere.com/
cnow/**

Refine your search using Boolean operators. Some search engines, like *AltaVista,* allow you to use the symbol '+', which means the same as "WITH". A search for "+dog biscuit recipes" would tell *AltaVista* to find documents *with* "dog" in them, combined with the optional other words like "biscuit" and "recipes". This will eliminate your getting websites for cheese biscuits and soda biscuit recipes because every document must contain the word "dog".

Similarly, you can use the "-" sign. A search for "wine recipes" using "-dandelion" would ensure that you would never be exposed to a recipe using that noxious weed.

If you have experimented with the Boolean operators and you're still not finding what you want, don't despair. You still have a number of tricks up your sleeve. You can always read the HELP that appears on every search engine page. Then again, you could try a different search engine. There are hundreds of them on the Internet.

Warrior Byte

Insanely Great Software has some interesting tools for serious Net researchers, including stock market quotations, domain name searcher, and weather and ski reports around the world. Check it out at: **http://igsnet.com/**

Each search engine tends to have a speciality. Some will search only Usenet newsgroups, some only for downloadable files. Others specialize in finding out the latest news or tracking down addresses. You will have to do some snooping of your own to find out which search engine is the best for your particular needs.

ADVANCED SEARCHING

Warrior Byte

Nothing like a ferret for ferreting out information. These programs are combined in a *suite*, which means you can take all of them or just the ones you're interested in. The *NetFerret* suite includes:

WebFerret—uses multiple search engines to locate the information on your topic, quickly and efficiently.

EmailFerret—a fast way to find anyone's E-mail address on the Internet. This ferret locates E-mail addresses of individuals, companies or robots.

IRCFerret—searches the Internet Relay Chat networks to locate anyone on any channel of the world's IRC networks.

Warrior Byte

Other programs in the *NetFerret* suite include:

FileFerret—searches and allows you to download all those interesting files and programs you want for your computer. If you only know the partial name of a file, the ferret can still find it.

NewsFerret—the fastest way to find and retrieve Usenet news articles on any topic. It is also a functional news-reading client.

PhoneFerret—finds the telephone numbers of individuals in the US by simply entering their name. You can install the Dialer software to automatically dial a retrieved number. For a free demo of the *Ferret Suite*, go to:

http://www.vironix.com/

One of the lesser-known tricks to successful information-gathering is the magic of FTP. FTP is *File Transfer Protocol*, which allows you to transfer information files to your computer by downloading. Long before the Internet became popular with the average citizen, it was used to store vital scientific information, statistics and data. In the event of a nuclear holocaust, the US Department of Defense would have a reliable communications network and scientists would be able to access data banks from anywhere in the world. What this means to you as an individual is that there are thousands of databases containing more information than you could possibly imagine. To access these data banks, all you have to do is type **ftp://** instead of **http://.**

To get a little help with FTP files, you should ask ARCHIE. Archie's name is short for "archive" because it searches database archives for you. Perhaps you know the name of a particular file you're looking for, but you haven't a clue where to locate it, or you can remember only a portion of the name. This is a case for ARCHIE. An Archie server stores a record of all the files at different FTP sites, a central registry of files. Your own service provider may have an Archie for you, or search the Net for one that you can use.

Warrior Byte

During your searches, you're bound to come across a message like "404 Error—Site Not Found." Like any neighborhood, the Internet is constantly changing. People move to different Internet Service Providers (ISPs). People marry, divorce and die. This activity determines the location of their web pages. Sometimes you find out what happened to a favorite page by downsizing the URL. For example, you might want to become a member of Microsoft's Internet Web designer team, but can't find exactly what you're looking for at the Internet address someone has given you.

**http://www.microsoft.com/sbnmember/
channels/**

could be downsized to:

http://www.microsoft.com/sbnmember/

or further to:

http://www.microsoft.com

By downsizing the original URL, you may access an index that will take you to the page you want.

Every Internet address has a *domain extension.* These will give you an idea of the type of information that may be stored in their data banks.

Conventional Domains		Proposed New Domains	
.com	commercial businesses	**.arts**	culture & entertainment
.edu	college & university sites	**.firm**	business sites
.gov	government organizations	**.info**	information providers
.int	international organizations (e.g. NATO)	**.nom**	personal home pages
.mil	military organizations	**.rec**	recreational sites
.net	large network companies	**.store**	sites that sell merchandise
.org	non-profit organizations	**.web**	sites about the Internet

Using FTP to snoop around, you'll be able to see what information different websites have stored in their publicly accessible files. FTP may give you the opportunity to research some elusive, lesser-known and less accessible information. This will be discussed in later chapters. A wealth of information is out there for the taking. Develop the skill to uncover it and you'll create your own wealth by marketing it!

Warrior Byte

Let a *Gopher* do your research work:

http://galaxy.einet.net/GJ/

Some research tools have gone out of fashion because people like the bells, whistles and animated graphics that web pages offer. Gopher may not have the toys you enjoy, but it gets the job done. Giving you unlimited access to the entire Internet, Gopher retrieves unique information through FTP, Archie, telnet and newsgroups. When the Internet first began to link millions of computers to gazillions of users, Gopher was created at the University of Minnesota, as one of the first search engines. It is still widely used to uncover information not available through other search engines.

Warrior Byte

Don't limit your searches to the World Wide Web engines when there are sophisticated search tools available. *Autonomy* is a company that has an extremely powerful, intelligent searching device that appears on your screen as a puppy. These puppies can be trained to source every piece of information available on any particular subject. It's like having your own personal librarian. *Autonomy Agents* (the puppies) search through newspapers and magazine articles as well, while you're busy doing more important things on the Internet. *Autonomy's Intelligent Agent* will scour the web looking for relevant documents to bring back to you.

Autonomy's Agentware™ Suite contains:

Web Researcher—enables you to research topics in-depth by locating relevant material throughout the World Wide Web and bringing it back to you.

> **Warrior Byte**
>
> Other programs in the **Agentware Suite**:
>
> **Press Office**—will create a personalized newspaper for you containing only those topics you're interested in. Information is gleaned from daily newspapers published on the web.
>
> **Image Researcher**—searches out the pictures and images that contain only what you've specified the Agent to retrieve from the Web, while eliminating logos and icons, unless requested.
>
> **Library**—builds an archive of retrieved documents on your PC for reading at your leisure.
>
> **Community**—for off-line searching, you can send your puppy to sniff out info while you sleep. Your vital material gets stored on a server until you are able to retrieve it. Your search agent will also contact other agents who are looking for similar information, allowing sharing of mutual interests.
>
> Want to give *Agentware Suite* a try? You can download it and try it free for 30 days:
>
> **http://agentware.com**

Some diverse (though often overlooked) sources of information come from your fellow human beings. If you are interested in a specific or obscure topic such as insect diseases, for example, you may be better off subscribing to a mailing list where you can cavort with like-minded insect disease aficionados.

Warrior Byte

Find out if a mailing list exists for your topic of interest. Here's a list by subject:

**http://salmosa.kaist.ac.kr/POINTER/
mailing-list-by-subject.html**

Try *Liszt*, the Mailing List Directory:

http://www.liszt.com

There are other specific lists like:

http://tile.net

Learn how to host your own mailing list:

http://www.lyris.com

Another, often overlooked way of getting first-hand information is the good, old-fashioned Bulletin Board System. Before the Internet caught on, many people ran BBSs on low-end computers set up in their bedrooms or garages. Bulletin Board Systems provide meeting places for individuals to make announcements, conduct discussion groups, share information and obtain services. Many of them contain a colossal number of files, utilities and games available for downloading. They often encourage participants to upload their own files or home-made programs.

BBSs run the gamut of topics and most of them are free. Some do, however, request a small fee to help defer the costs of keeping them going. There are even some *for profit* systems, particularly those that specialize in erotica or popular games. Some require specialized software (usually available free) to make full use of their services. Most of them allow you access using a simple telnet program, which is a very basic program that allows you to connect to another computer through a modem. Simply by typing in commands, you immediately receive printed results on the screen. It's fun and interesting to own your own BBS and information on set-up is readily available.

If you are using Windows95 as your operating system, you have telnet capability built right into your computer. Click on your START button on the lower left of your screen. Choose RUN and then type *telnet* in the OPEN field. Hit the OKAY button and a telnet screen will open up for you. Connect using the domain name provided by the particular Bulletin Board. There is a HELP section built into the program, so it won't take long for you to catch on.

For BBSs that require you to phone in directly, your Windows95 has a *hyperterminal program*, which works essentially the same way as telnet. Again, click on START, then go to PROGRAMS, ACCESSORIES and choose the file HYPERTERMINAL. Open HYPER-TRM.EXE and follow the instructions on the screen to place your first call.

If you want access to libraries and databases that are not available on the World Wide Web, use your hyperterminal program to dial up your regular Internet Service Provider. Log on with your password and then look for HYTELNET. You won't be able to use your mouse, so it takes a bit of getting used to. In most cases, if you type the word *help* and hit the ENTER key, you will get some help. Most sessions can be ended by typing the word *quit*. The joy of hytelnet is that it takes you to sources of information that haven't been coded into pages that are viewable by your web browser. Hytelnet will take you to Internet-accessible libraries, freenets, BBSs and places only approachable by telnet. This is a snooper's paradise!

Warrior Byte

The Mother of all BBSs is a comprehensive list of bulletin boards for topics throughout the world:

http://wwwmbb.cs.colorado.edu/~mcbryan/ bb/summary.html

If you would like to run your own BBS, stop here first and learn how to run a better BBS:

http://www.thedirectory.org/diamond/runbbs.htm

Newsgroups are a terrific way to gain information and make contacts. It would be well worth your while to learn how to use a news reader program such as Free Agent that can provide you with help and download a list of all the active newsgroups your service provider has access to. There are over twenty thousand different newsgroups discussing anything from celebrity gossip to rocket fuel. Collaborations happen daily as a result of this sharing of ideas.

The World Wide Web provides access to people and libraries on a global scale. What a gold mine! At this point in time, only a small fraction of the population is tapping this phenomenal resource—let one of them be you!

Warrior Byte

Speciality search sites include:

AltaVista—http://www.altavista.digital.com

A number of unique features attract people to this search engine. To make sure that a specific word is in the document you're searching for, type a '+' sign in front. If you're searching for raspberry wine recipes, for example, try *+raspberry wine recipes*. This ensures that the word *raspberry* appears in every document. To learn how to use AltaVista (or any search engine) efficiently, read the help section. AltaVista lets you know how many web pages are hooked up to your web page. For example:

link:http://www.netscape.com shows you how many people have a reference to the Netscape network on their pages. To peruse the pages at a particular site, type: **host:the.siteURL** in the search field.

Warrior Byte

Another specialty search site:

DejaNews

http://www.dejanews.com/home_ps.shtml

This is a great search engine to use to find out the latest gossip on your favorite celebrity. By typing in your celeb's name, you can access all the newsgroups where others are dropping the same name. Try it and see what you can learn. Another trick with DejaNews is discovering all the postings a person has made to different newsgroups just by clicking on their E-mail address. Use it to find out the secret interests and hobbies of your friends, by seeing what newsgroups they monitor. Try clicking on the different links. When you want to get back to your original search, click your BACK button.

This is a small sampling of search engines. The list is endless. The best advice I can give you is to try various engines until you find what you're looking for. The more proficient you become in your search, the more productive your Internet time will be.

Now that you're armed with a little information, let's put it to work making money for you.

CHAPTER FOUR

A COMPUTER CAN MAKE YOU MONEY

■ ■ ■ ■ ■ ■ ■

hat's all this about, anyway? You may have picked up this book out of curiosity. It you don't already own a computer or don't have an Internet connection, then reading through this book should convince you that you're missing out on some serious action. You don't need to break your piggy bank to get in on the action, either.

You can get your mitts on the Internet goodies with an old 386 PC and a 14,400 modem. If you're a novice, you probably don't know what any of this means but basically, it's the bare minimum system to get you connected. If you intend to print out any of the pertinent material you find on the Net, a letter-quality, dot-matrix printer should do just fine. You should be able to get up and running for under $500.

There are plenty of books and magazines to help you find your first computer. *Cyberspeak* will certainly sound like a foreign language to you initially, but don't let that scare you off. All you need to know is how to point and click a mouse. Do your research—talk to friends and colleagues who own computers. Make a point of being a knowledgeable consumer so that you are not oversold, especially on an introductory system.

Step into the water slowly. Once you know the depth and the temperature, you can slip in all the way with confidence and thoroughly enjoy the swim.

Of course, you'll bring your new computer home and not have a clue where to start. You and your monitor will stare at each other blankly until you get up the courage to touch the on/off switch, boot up your hard drive, link arms and make your way cautiously through cyberspace together. Consider a couple of classes at your local community college so that you can get to know your computer intimately.

If you're fortunate enough to have a teenager in your neighborhood, a lot of your start-up problems will be over. You'll find that obscure techno-gene implanted firmly into most kids nowadays. They've had a keyboard in their mitts since kindergarten and they love to show you what they know. You'll find their enthusiasm contagious and they'll get you set up and connected before you've even figured out where the electric plug goes. Although this book doesn't advocate that you exploit children, teenage computer buffs work dirt-cheap. If you don't have cash, you're bound to have a few things around the house to make your young employee's eyes sparkle. Start with free cola and pizza and negotiate from there.

Assuming you've overcome the first few obstacles to getting started, have a look at some of the computer opportunities available on the Internet. You've probably heard a lot of hype about the Internet and all it can do for you. The Internet is a major economic force in the business world on a global scale. All commercial transactions can take place in cyberspace, using only a credit card and a computer. Money can be exchanged for goods and services anywhere in the world and there is very little any government can do to control it.

Back on the home front, you probably bought this book because you wanted to learn a little bit about the Internet and its relevance to your own life. If you're a business person, you will no doubt be hiring staff and taking professional development courses to learn how to get your business wired. If you want to set up your own Internet Service Provider, you will have to hit the technical books, but if you're looking for "just enough cash" to feed your newly-acquired Internet habit, this book will accommodate you.

YOUR OWN WEB PAGE—AN IDEA BANK

Warrior Byte

Don't want to learn how to make a web page? Then let someone else's computer generate one for you. Here's a place to start:

Keypals Club:
**http://www.worldkids.net/clubs/kci/
home page.html**

> **Warrior Byte**
>
> Additional places to look for web designers:
>
> *Webspawner:*
>
> **http://www.webspawner.com**
>
> *Town Square 2000:*
>
> **http://townsquare.usr.com**

There is money to be made in web page design, but it's a jungle out there and you need skills that will set you apart from the rest. Unless you specialize in animation or web security, you won't make tons of money. Nonetheless, anyone can learn the basics and develop enough proficiency to design pages for others as well as themselves. There are an overwhelming number of free software programs that will guide you through the fundamentals and let you produce a fairly decent product. If you have any degree of artistic ability, your pages will look better than 95% of those currently on the web. To determine your hourly or per page rate, call around and get estimates from other designers. For initial exposure, offer to design a web page for free for your favorite local charity.

As you're surfing the Net, you'll notice many home pages have advertising banners on top. Advertisers will pay people to display their logo and direct viewers to their site. Often, the income generated this way is enough to cover your monthly Internet expenses. Don't overlook this source of immediate income. Your spouse would probably be very happy if you could cover your $20/month ISP (Internet Service Provider) fee.

Warrior Byte

For a list of advertisers who will pay to advertise on your website, go to:

http://www.markwelch.com/bannerad/

How do you attract visitors to your web page? That's easy—*give something away!* The most popular sites are offering free software, graphics, animation, jokes, celebrity addresses and information on where to get free stuff. If you have programming skills, artistic talent, research or other skills, you can probably think of a few freebies to offer on your own web page. Everyone has something of value that they can share with others—ie. recipes, patterns or information on how to do almost anything. Become a true cyber citizen and contribute to the world. If we all shared our ideas and were open to learning from each other, maybe we'd get along better with each other locally and globally.

Another way to attract visitors to your site is to set up a *Meta Resource.* This is an Internet website that people can use for a general reference. It contains links to everything on the Internet pertaining to a particular subject. It attracts people because it makes their searching easier when everything's listed on one page. It takes a bit of time to find all the links that are relevant to your subject, but once your page becomes known as a good reference site, you'll get lots of repeat visitors. Set up a page containing *Everything You Need to Know About Raising Sea Monkeys* and you'll get hobbyists coming back again and again.

Your site can become very hot very fast if you have a contest. Use the newsgroups and search engines to invite people over to your site for a chance to win a T-shirt with your company logo on it. Get them to leave their name and address and fill in a brief form about their hobbies and interests. You'll be able to develop a database from this information to use for future marketing.

There are a number of ways that you can use your web page-making skills to earn extra money. Have you thought of hosting a site that displays students' writing or artwork? Set up a site to show off the special talents of different members of a Boy Scout/Girl Guide troop or local choir. As you well know, parents are very proud of their children's accomplishments. Just think what it would do for the self-esteem of a child to see his work displayed worldwide! What parent wouldn't be willing to spend $10 to have their child's work exhibited for a month on the Internet?

What about local groups? Would everyone in the local art club pay to have their artwork scanned and displayed with information on how to purchase? Consider the antique car collectors' club—perhaps they have automobiles that they want to sell to customers world-wide? With your web page-making skills, set up a site to showcase these valuable antiques. With your search skills, go to the appropriate newsgroup and approach potential customers or post the relevant information.

There are people all over the world who are selling their home-made crafts via the Internet. There are quilt patterns, woodworking patterns, language courses, home exchanges and bed-and-breakfast operations—so

many diverse services that you are bound to find someone locally who can use your Internet skills to put them
in touch with the rest of the world. Go for it!

Warrior Byte

Want to get serious about building web pages?
Hyper Text Mark-up Language is what you must
use to create pages that are recognized by most
web browsers.

- HTML editors can make creating a web page
  easy for any amateur:
  http://www.win.net/web_info/editors.html

- Want to learn more? There are literally thousands of sites to teach you how to produce professional quality web pages. Try this one:
  **http://www.geocities.com/EnchantedForest/
  2618/make_homepg.html**

- A Beginner's Guide to HTML:
  **http://www.ncsa.uiuc.edu/General/Internet/
  WWW/HTMLPrimer.html**

- Web Mastery has news forums and resource lists
  to help you overcome any problem:
  http://www.umr.edu/~oldfield/webmastery/

- Learn something new, like JAVA:
  http://www.wsabstract.com/

- How do they do that with HTML?
  **http://union.ncsa.uiuc.edu/HperNews/get/
  www/html/guides.html**

- Find out everything about everybody who's ever
  visited your web page. How to use legal and
  illegal HTML: **http://webtools.org/**

BECOMING AN EXPERT

Warrior Byte

Make exciting, cutting-edge pages by learning how to do animation for fun and profit. Here's where to start:

**http://www.acute.com/promote/graphics/
1gifani.htm**

and here's where to learn more:

http://members.aol.com/royalef/toolbox.htm

For the ultimate in tips, tricks and graphics, check out the *Ultimatorium*:

**http://www.pacificcoast.net/~mudhoney/
psycho2.htm**

There is a market for quality graphics and animations. Promote and sell your creations. One place that will buy graphics is:

http://members.xoom.com/royjay/

The *Animated Gif Artists Guild* can help with any questions you have:

http://www.agag.com/

Much of the technical knowledge that pertains to the Internet is still in its infancy stage. People just like you are learning their craft by trial and error, in the privacy of their own homes. No frame of reference exists for the Internet. If you take the time to learn to use a graphics program and an animation program, you will be considered an expert in the web page design field. You don't need to go to college to get the basics—all you need is the patience to read the manuals and do the tutorials that come with any program you purchase or download. Imagine how much smarter everyone would be if they did this! Most people can't be bothered and are happy to pay someone else who has the initiative to learn.

Warrior Byte

Make a screen saver for yourself or your friends. It's a great promotional product for your business. *Screen Paver* is a nifty little program that lets you set up a slide show of up to one hundred JPEG images for use as a screen saver. A free demo is available from:

http://www.download.com

or from the author at

http://tni.net/~mlindell/ScreenPaver.html

Make a rotating cube screen saver that displays your company's logo and related photographs. Download *Fotocube* by searching here:

http://www.hotfiles.com/

or from the developer here

http://www.lucidnumerics.com/fotocube/ index.html

Remember: if you enjoy using these products, please pay the authors. They work hard to develop these programs and must compete against big software companies.

Warrior Byte

N.B. A JPEG is a type of photo image formatting that can be viewed by web browsers. A scanner will turn your photographs into JPEG images that can be stored on disk or uploaded to the Internet. Many places that develop photos can also provide scanning services. Another format that allows pictures to be viewed in your web browser is GIF. *To find out more about JPEG and GIF, use the Internet glossary mentioned in the Warrior Byte on page 4.*

Once you've developed some degree of proficiency, you'll think of ways to profit from it. Get yourself to the library and learn how to sell yourself or find a website with this info. Learn how to find out where to locate customers and how to target them. Look in your yellow pages and newspaper want-ads to evaluate the competition and improve on what they're doing. When you know something that no one else knows, you've got a valuable (and marketable) asset. Your age, sex, race, religion or physical abilities have no bearing whatsoever on the marketability of your product, so don't let anything deter you!

Much of the software available now is so user-friendly it can make anyone look brilliant. It's impossible not to put it to work for you and make money.

> **Warrior Byte**
>
> How would you like to be able to get inside
> someone else's computer to view, use and repair
> their files without ever leaving your home?
> *Carbon Copy* lets you do it:
>
> **http://www.microcom.com/cc/cc.htm**

TUTORING

Once you've gained some degree of expertise and
confidence (not necessarily mastering a program), you
can teach what you've learned to others. This becomes
another source of income!

The general population is very hungry for this
knowledge—teach others how to connect to the
Internet, use an E-mail program, navigate using one of
the major web browsers, create a web page, create
graphics and animation, access all those informative
newsgroups, participate in CHAT groups or play interactive games... the list is as broad and varied as the
Internet itself. With a little time and attention to detail,
you can quickly become an *Internet Guru!*

If you can present ideas clearly, in an easy-to-follow
format, you can teach others what you know. Do so on
a consultant basis and you will not need the teaching
certificate that you would need through the school system. You can, however, acquire a recognized degree in
many areas via the Internet itself, through various
accredited universities. In fact, some very specialized

courses and seminars are offered by big computer corporations like Microsoft and are only available through
the Internet. You can upgrade your own qualifications
while helping others learn more!

Warrior Byte

Don't let age or a physical disability prevent you
from attaining your education goals. Learn in your
own home, on your own time.

The Electronic University Network provides fully
accredited college and university education entirely on-line. Their on-line campus provides courses,
libraries and support services, including a student
union for socializing, buying books and university
paraphernalia:

http://www.wcc-eun.com/

Distance Education Facilities allow you to experience education worldwide for an eclectic learning experience. Never boring, they utilize novel
methods to attend to your needs:

**http://ccism.pc.athabascau.ca/html/ccism/
deresrce/institut.htm**

American Institute of Computer Sciences—just
one of many virtual campuses:

http://www.aics.edu

Distance Education Guru—a list of excellent
resources for improving your mind. These Internet
universities and training institutes give you professional, recognized degrees and training courses to
advance your career credentials. Continuing professional education is arranged through mail, FAX,
modem, and on-line means:

http://home.rmci.net/michael/index6.htm

Show other people how they can benefit by assimilating this new technology. Here are some venues for teaching Internet courses:

- Evening courses at your local community college or public school
- Seniors' clubs and youth clubs
- Special interest groups and hobbyists
- Summer camps
- Private lessons in your home or in someone else's
- Trade shows
- Computer stores (as part of their sales package)
- Your ISP (Internet Service Provider)

SETTING UP OTHER SURFERS

Warrior Byte

Who needs the Internet? Everybody! Are you lonesome tonight? Join in a rousing game of bridge with partners three thousand miles away:
http://www.passport2.com

BINGO! It's FREE!:
http://www.bingozone.com

Listen to radio stations around the world:
http://www.ontheair.com

Are your typing fingers tired? Try chatting with someone on the next continent using one of these voice programs:
http://www.onlive.com

If your friends and neighbors aren't wired to the Net, they don't know what they're missing! Help these underpriviledged people and generate some extra cash. It won't take long to learn how to install the software that most ISPs give to new customers. You can charge for your time or volunteer your services to help others get connected. While you're helping out, you can leave a business card, offering private lessons for newcomers.

Don't forget to barter! Your set-up knowledge is worth something. Trade the time you spent connecting your neighbor's kids to the Internet for their lawn-mowing services. Hook up granny and reap some home-made wine. Swap tools, software, house-cleaning, whatever. Money isn't the only form of exchange in this world!

Many Internet Service Providers give you extra free access time when you get someone else to sign up. This is a small bonus that helps to pay for your own Internet habit. Once you gain proficiency and learn more about computers, you will have the confidence to set up small businesses...which can become another source of income for you and help to grow the Internet in your community.

DOMAIN NAMES

Warrior Weapon

Remember domain name extensions are listed on page 45.

Sooner or later you (or someone you know) will want to obtain a domain name for your exclusive use. It's easier for people to remember a simple name that will take them to your website. A domain name makes it easy for your customers to find you on the Net. Major companies like Microsoft have their own domains—all you have to do is type the word *Microsoft* into the location field of your web browser and there you are! With other browsers, you will have to type **http://www.microsoft.com.** Either way, it makes the Microsoft Company very easy to find.

Two-letter domain names, which correspond to countries, require a different set of rules. For example, to register a Canadian national company (which would give you the ending .CA), you would have to apply to the CA domain committee. (At the time of this writing, CA names are free and are only available to federally, provincially or municipally-registered companies).

Warrior Byte

In Canada, you can apply for a CA domain at:

**ftp://ftp.cs.utoronto.ca/registry/
application-form**

To find out where to register a two-letter domain name in other countries, go here:

http://www.uninett.no/navn/domreg.html

Applying for a domain name is not difficult. For conventional domains (e.g. Those ending in .COM or .ORG), you must use the InterNIC. *The Internet Network Information Centre* is a database and directory server run by AT&T, National Science Foundation and Network Solutions. It provides a registry for all domain names and network numbers.

Anyone who is willing to pay US$50/year can qualify for a commercial (.COM) domain name. Here are the basic steps:

1. Choose a few prospective names and do a WHOIS search through the InterNIC records for each name to determine whether or not the name is already in use.

2. Once you've chosen a name, notify your service provider. Many ISPs will handle the name registration for you for a small fee. Your service provider has to know about your domain name, whether they do the registration or not. Otherwise, your Internet connection may not work, nor will you receive E-mail.

3. Fill out the proper application form in cooperation with your service provider. (The forms are available on-line.)

4. You will usually be informed within 1-2 weeks regarding the acceptance of your application.

> **Warrior Byte**
>
> To find out if anyone else is using the name you want, check *WHOIS:*
>
> **http://rs.internic.net/cgi-bin/whois**
>
> Learn more about domain names and apply for your own at:
>
> **http://rs.internic.net/index2.html**
>
> **http://rs.internic.net/domain-info/ internic-domain-6.html**
>
> **http://rs.internic.net/cgi-bin/itts/domain**

Once you have established your own domain name, you can host other people's pages at your site for a small fee. Most Internet Service Providers permit business customers to purchase more space, as needed, inexpensively. This allows you to set up and display web pages that you've designed for others.

> **Warrior Byte**
>
> For those of you who don't like the *InterNIC* monopoly, try an alternative domain registry:
>
> **http://www.alternic.net/**

> **Warrior Byte**
>
> For those of you who dream of having your own domain name but want to avoid the expense, consider using a site that starts with **travel.to** or **surf.to** or **come.to**. This can be a clever way of having a memorable domain name without the bother. To find out how this works, go to:
>
> **http://come.to**

Once you're up and running on the Net, it's important to announce to the world that you've arrived. Take the time to submit your website to all the various search engines. People who are searching for the goods and services you offer will be able to find you easily if you get yourself linked to as many related sites as possible. Do everything imaginable to increase your exposure and your web traffic. Follow tips offered by the experts and your site will quickly generate E-mail inquiries.

> **Warrior Byte**
>
> *Addme* allows you to submit your website to thirty-five popular search engines, for free:
>
> **http://www.addme.com/**
>
> Increase you web traffic with many tips and tricks supplied at:
>
> **http://www.submit-it.com/**
>
> Business sites—get a free link at:
>
> **http://www.bargainseeker.com/**

CHAPTER FIVE

HELP YOURSELF

■ ■ ■ ■ ■ ■

If you've read this far, you already have a small taste of the boundless and delicious opportunities the Internet has to offer. Consider this:

- Where else can you get the most current information on *any* subject *instantaneously?* This is the Information Age and the Net is the most efficient, cost-effective means to access and circulate information. It's a fast-paced world and the quickest route to knowledge and success is on the Information Highway.

- Where else can you keep your eye on the competition, not only locally, but globally? If you're not aware of what the competition is doing, how can you possibly compete?

- Where else can you share the collective brainpower of thousands? New ideas, new inventions, new philosophies are what keep the world turning and the economy churning. Don't suffer from stagnation and brain-rot. Find out what's happening! Share in the synergy—grow and contribute!

- Where else can you get so much for so little? The Internet is cheap entertainment, often costing less than $1/hour.

- Where else can you access all the services of your post office at the push of a button?...all the services provided by your phone company at 1/10 the cost?...the facilities of the largest research centre in the world? Cheap! Cheap! Cheap!

- Where else can you meet new friends who live thousands of miles away?

- Where else can you experience, first-hand, different perspectives on a news story or share your culture and ideas through instant on-line chat?

- Where else can you access free education anytime—day or night?

The Internet makes the whole world your playground. Internet experts tell us that by the year 2000 there will be more than 200 million people connected from almost every country in the world. Think of the possibilities!

Warrior Byte

Do you have something to sell on the Internet? *Here's a valuable tip—being authorized to take Visa or Mastercard, will instantly increase your sales by 30%.* Customers will buy on impulse because they can fill in your form right away, without taking time to send a check or money order in the mail.

GOING INTO BUSINESS

> **Warrior Byte**
>
> How does a small business go about setting up a merchant account? There are a number of agents and solicitors who can get your application approved. Shop around and compare fees. Some places that handle credit shopping are:
>
> **http://www.creditcards-atm.com/**
>
> and
>
> **http://www.merchantaccount.com/**
>
> Do a search using the key words *credit cards* or *merchant accounts* or *merchant account credit cards* to reveal credit card sites.

Perhaps the most complicated part of any business venture is its start-up. Where do other people come up with profitable business ideas? The Internet is *bursting* with them!

Every successful entrepreneur knows that a good idea needs a good business plan. Check out the thousands of business reports available on the Net for novice entrepreneurs. These reports cover topics such as *Survival Tips for Small Businesses, How to Accomplish Anything You Want In Life, The Layperson's Crash Course in Business Credit, How to Borrow Your Way to Wealth* and much, much more. It's beyond the scope of this book to examine the content of each report in any detail, but the information is out there and I can show you how to access it. Once you start digging, you'll pull out all the stops and pull together all the pieces you need to develop a dynamite business plan.

If you already have an E-mail account, you've probably received a cart-load of offers from firms who want to "help you get started" in your own business. They usually try to sell you an information package for $20 or more. NOTE: This information is available for FREE if you know where to look. In fact, why not use your own research skills to uncover information for *other* businesses and charge *them* for your time? Do it better than the other guys!

It would be foolish to limit yourself to information from one source. The Internet gives you unlimited access to worldwide knowledge! Before you invest time and money in any idea, you owe it to yourself to uncover as much information as possible. Make some inquiries, determine which businesses are reputable and which have complaints lodged against them. Ask in newsgroups and during chat sessions. Use the Internet to its full potential.

Warrior Byte

If you're dreaming of being in business for yourself but don't know where to start, the Internet is a diamond mine for ideas. Start with these free reports that contain exciting moneymaking ideas:

http://www.icemall.com/reports/index.html

> **Warrior Byte**
>
> Here's another site that contains over a thousand free reports on small business and personal finance:
>
> **http:/www.insiderreports.com/**
>
> Save yourself a lot of time and aggravation by learning from the mistakes of others. Check out *World Internet Insolvency & Bankruptcy Resources* and learn what not to do:
>
> **http://www.insolvency.com/**

MAILING LABELS

> **Warrior Weapon**
>
> To obtain a news browser like Free Agent (available free), check the warrior byte on page 36. This news browser has a help section that will show you how to search for specific newsgroups.

With a little research, you can compile your own database, by interest group, and sell these market-specific "mailing lists" to other companies. By targeting specific interest groups, you've cornered a particular market—for instance, people interested in travel. It's easy to create a precise mailing list:

1. Go into a news browser like Free Agent. Do a search for all newsgroups pertaining to travel and you will come across the following: **alt.travel, alt.travel.canada, alt.travel.eurail, alt.travel.roadtrip, alt.travel.eurail.youth-hostels,** and so on.

2. Subscribe to those newsgroups that target a specific market and download a day's worth of news. (Be sure to go off-line while you read through the information. Remember: the meter is running while you're on-line).

3. Read each posting. Most participants in a newsgroup have an E-mail address or a signature at the end of their letter. Keep track of these names and E-mail addresses.

4. Work backward, using a good people-finder search engine. Once you have an E-mail address, you can find out a person's mailing address and postal code.

Warrior Byte

There are a number of places on the Internet that conduct people searches. Once you have a list of names, your next step would be to go to:

http://www.search.com

Do a PEOPLE search to get their street addresses and postal codes. For worldwide listings, try:

http:///www.whowhere.com/wwphone/world. html

FINGER is a simple program that will provide you with a person's real name from their E-mail address. Some service providers disable this program to provide privacy for their users, but many ISPs put out a profile on their users, which includes their full name and, sometimes, their occupation and hobbies. This can be helpful when compiling your mailing label list and makes cross-referencing your database simple and easy. Eudora Pro has this program built right into its TOOLS, DIRECTORY SERVICES. There are FINGER programs available throughout the Internet and profiles can also be accessed through TELNET.

> **Warrior Byte**
>
> For more information on FINGER, try:
>
> **http://help.west.net/accman/finger.html**

Compiling mailing lists is time-consuming, but once you have the initial database, you can sell your list to companies looking for specific consumers. Lists of names and addresses are printed on self-adhering labels, and sold to companies directly or through a broker. To find out more about the mailing list business, search the Internet and read some of the business reports available.

> **Warrior Byte**
>
> How do you find a broker to sell your mailing list?
>
> **http://www.thebiz.co.uk/marmai.htm**

WORKING FROM HOME

Home-based businesses can be a tremendous advantage for many people. Here are a few of the reasons:

- You may have a physical disability that makes travel difficult.

- You may have children who require your presence in the home.

- You have examined the tax advantages that owning your own home business can offer.

- You want to work your own hours, at your own convenience.

- You want to avoid the high overhead that running an office business entails.

- You hate driving through congested streets and then fighting for over-priced, elusive parking spaces...or you just plain hate commuting.

Join the ranks of thousands of other people who work, either part-time or full-time from their homes. If you have the self-discipline to remain motivated in spite of many temptations and distractions, you'll enjoy the liberation that home employment brings. It's important that you approach self-employment with the same dedication and respect that you would working away from home.

> **Warrior Byte**
>
> Many Netters are leaving the hustle and bustle of the office for a small cubicle in their own homes. There are plenty of Internet sites to help you stay motivated while on your own—avoid the feeling of isolation that can sometimes seep in and stay connected with the outside world. *The National Home Workers Association* is full of ideas and articles:
>
> **http://www.homeworkers.com/**
>
> Here is a site that is dedicated to helping parents who want to stay home and raise their children, but still need two incomes:
>
> **http://pw2.netcom.com/~hgrady/home.html**
>
> *The National Association for the Self-Employed* is dedicated to helping you be a successful entrepreneur:
>
> **http://selfemployed.nase.org/NASE/**

BARTER

Good, old-fashioned barter is fast becoming the currency of the future. Why on earth would any business want to exchange goods or services and miss out on the delightful jingle of nickel and copper?

Barter is an actual growth industry, generating billions in revenue. Surely you want to have a piece of this action? It's no longer relegated to local neighborhood bazaars and has become wired to the Internet. Businesses can find an immediate taker for their surplus products as well as take advantage of goods and services offered by other on-line businesses.

You don't have to exchange bottle caps for chickens, which are later exchanged for truck tires, in order to bring home the bacon you need for your family. Your goods and services are valued in *cyber dollars,* which are exchangeable for someone else's products. Cyber dollars are a convenient electronic unit of exchange that is not legal tender but is used for barter.

By joining a barter community, you can make new contacts, solicit potential customers for your products and meet new trading partners.

Warrior Byte

You can enjoy the business of bartering anywhere. Barter with other businesses worldwide:

http://www.clubmagenta.com/barter.htm

http://www.activeinternational.com/

Barter federally (includes Canada and Mexico):

http://www.barter.com/

http://www.itexbarterworks.com/

Barter locally:

http://www.tradebanc.com/CreativeBarter.html

BUY, SELL AND SECOND-HAND

The Internet is bursting with merchandise of all sorts. There are thousands of Internet malls where you can buy and sell absolutely anything! Do a search for "Internet Mall" and you'll be stuck to your computer screen for hours. This is a tremendous opportunity to obtain goods and services at a price that's affordable for you, whether for your own use or for resale. Show the world your stuff!

Let's say you're in the market for a reasonable second-hand computer for someone who requires specialized software necessary to enhance his cyber business, but the $1,500 price tag is a little hefty. He may want to trade his old 386 for a newer 486DX66. Can you do this deal over the Internet? You bet! Use your search skills to find "used computers", "used software" and the old stand-bys "trade" and "swap".

> **Warrior Byte**
>
> Want to trade in your old computer? Try the on-line used computer swap:
>
> **http://www.creativelement.com/swap/**
>
> If you actually have some cash on hand, it wouldn't hurt to check out *The United Computer Exchange Corporation*, a global clearinghouse for buyers and sellers of new and used micro-computer equipment:
>
> **http://www.uce.com/**

> **Warrior Byte**
>
> If you need some fancy software for that computer you just purchased, pay a visit to the used software site:
>
> **http://www.midwinter.com/usox/**
>
> Or try *Embryo* at:
>
> **http://www.embryo.com/**

What's more fun than an auction? At auction sites on the Internet, place your bid on the object of your desire. As others see what you've bid, they enter their own bids. This continues for a set period of time, after which all bids are final. If you're lucky, you may be the proud owner of a color flatbed scanner for a mere $30! It happens every day.

There are hundreds of reputable auction sites— many operating as clearing houses for brand new, surplus goods from recognized companies. Do a search for *auctions*, specifying the particular item you want. There are *real estate auctions, computer auctions, government surplus auctions, police seizure auctions,* even *bicycle, boat* or *livestock auctions.* I can't list all of the various types of auctions; embark on your exciting Internet search and discover a world of auction possibilities.

Try running your own auction site for speciality items. Visit some of the established auction sites and see how they arrange bidding. If you have quality merchandise to sell and conduct your business in a professional manner, you won't have any problem attracting bidders. Network with people in your community to see if they have antiques, arts and crafts, sports equipment or whatever and determine the potential. You'll have to do some research to find out about export laws, tax laws and standard commission rates, but this information is available at your fingertips...where else? On the Internet.

Warrior Byte

If you're considering the auction biz, a little legal advice would be appropriate. Personalized legal advice is available at:

http://www.cyberlegal.com/

Become familiar with the workings of an actual Internet auction. Bid on products or sell your own. All the excitement of a live auction at:

http://www.bidnask.com/

Don't forget to do a little on-line haggling while you're at:

http://www.haggle.com

This auction site claims to be the world's largest:

http://pages.ebay.com/aw/index.html

Bidaway will accept just about any item for auction. Those not connected to the Internet can place bids or sell items using conventional methods like fax, phone and snail mail:

http://www.bidaway.com/

There are many more auction sites you can explore, so do a little surfing.

You can make a tidy profit buying foreclosures but be sure to do your research prior to investing. In every country, in every single state or province or county, there are foreclosures happening (situations in which someone has not paid their taxes or mortgage, for one reason or another, and their bank has taken their home away from them). A smart buyer can step in and make a tidy profit. Be familiar with this particular real estate market before you jump in with your hard-earned dollars. Become knowledgeable on the subject and then approach with caution. There are foreclosure software programs available on the Internet that will help you determine the fair market value for a particular building or house. Calculations are done for you so that you won't be purchasing in the dark. Do an Internet search for *foreclosure software* and choose one that meets your needs. Once you've learned a little about the foreclosure business, you can search the Internet for foreclosure news, newsletters and information.

Warrior Byte

There is an Internet magazine that lists foreclosures all over the United states at:

http://www.foreclosure-mag.com

National Foreclosures On-Line is another place to research this business:

http://www.nationalforeclosures.com/

as well as the *National Foreclosure Network* at:

http://www.hipstuff.com/ForeclosureNet/ index.htm

FREE FOR THE SEARCHING

Warrior Byte

HELP YOURSELF! You've got nothing to lose by entering every contest available on or off the Internet. Just about every contest that exists is listed at:

http://contest.catalogue.com/contest/ contests/html

You're a potential millionaire!

Nothing brightens your day more than getting something for nothing and it's completely impossible to surf the Net without finding some free stuff. It's a cheapskate's paradise.

Not only can you get enough free software to freeze up your hard drive forever, you can get free advice from licensed practitioners and tradespeople, free services delivered right to your doorstep and free samples of everything from soup to soap. Go to one of your favorite search engines and type *free sample of tobacco* and see what turns up. If that doesn't work, try another search engine. Ask members of a newsgroup or chat room where you can get a free sample of tobacco. With a bit of warrior ingenuity you can indulge your habit for half of what you're currently paying.

You can get *free trial subscriptions* to enough magazines to crush your postman. There are ample *free vitamins* to get our heart pumping double time and sufficient *free sex aids* to give Superman a hernia. Make it your mission in life to get something for nothing every day of the year!

Warrior Byte

The Internet is loaded with free software, advice and services. Here's one of the first places to stop—*Bubba's Bazaar*—a bargain hunter's oasis on the web:

http://www.intro.net/free.html

You want shareware? Type the word:

http://www.shareware.com

Free home pages, free E-mail addresses, free publicity, free screen savers, free software, free images, free midis, free…

http://www.freebyte.com/

Some of the most unusual (as well as practical) free stuff is listed here:

http://www.bright.net/~booters/lotsfree.htm

REAL ESTATE

Many people are hesitant to invest in real estate because they think they need a lot of money to get started. They've invariably heard some horror story about someone who purchased a money pit that ruined their finances and cost them their marriage. In spite of the perceived danger, there are more people who have made big money in real estate than from any other form of investment. There are a number of ways to make money in real estate; buying foreclosures, fixer-uppers or mortgages, to name a few.

What you need, before jumping into the real estate market, is a good education. There are info-mercials that claim anyone can make a million in real estate by taking a special course. There are also courses that enable people to become licensed Realtors. If you plan to *dabble* in real estate, however, all the information you need is available for free on the Internet. Build the necessary skills, make your contacts and even advertise using the resources available on the World Wide Web.

Warrior Byte

People are making fortunes in real estate. Even if you haven't got a cent, all you need is the knowledge. Why pay for fancy courses when one of the best sites for providing a proper education in real estate is available free. Connect to the Internet and download the reports you need:

http://www.real-estate-on-line.com/

FINDER'S FEES

There is big money for those who take the time to source a customer base for specific clients. These opportunities are so often overlooked that any person with a little ambition and know-how can bring in great rewards. Many small businesses will pay a reward if you can connect them with someone who meets their needs. If they successfully negotiate a transaction as a result of your contact, you'll receive cash or merchandise for your effort. Start your Internet search using *finder's fee* or *reward*. The number of sites that turn up from a simple search is mind-boggling. No matter where you live, there are opportunities in finder's fees.

Finder's fees are paid to anyone who can bring in collections such as records, CDs, coins or comics. Large fees can be made in real estate by connecting a buyer with a seller or a renter with a tenant. Connecting with the right employee is valuable to an employer. People looking for sources of venture capital will pay for contacts and web providers are always looking for customers. Immigrant investors are looking for investments that will give them legal status in the country of their choice; offshore banks want more customers for their services. The list is *endless*.

Warrior Byte

Here are a few ideas to get you started in the lucrative finder's fee business:

Find people who are receiving monthly payments from personal injury lawsuits, estates, trusts, lotteries etc. Many companies will give them a lump sum amount of money in exchange for their monthly payoffs. Examples of such places are:

**http://www2.setcap.com/WEBSITES/
SetCap/home.htm**

and

http://integrityfunding.net/

There is an *Immigrant Investors Visa Program*:

http://www.conexxus.com/

A number of small and larger businesses will pay you to find customers for their software, machinery, graphics or web page production:

http://members.tripod.com/~MoneyML/

This company purchases other companies and will pay for referrals:

**http://www.lumonix.com/pmg/
commissions.html**

Consider aggressively finding things for your friends and neighbors. Perhaps someone you know needs a special type of software program and doesn't have the time to search for it or the inclination to install it themselves. Provide this service for a fee. There are many people earning substantial incomes from finder's fees alone. Suppose your cousin is looking for a new car or your sister wants a puppy for the kids. Instead of restricting their search locally, advertise worldwide for them on the Net. Charge them for your time as you advertise in various newsgroups. Charge for your knowledge, if you advertise, by creating a web page for them or charge a finder's fee if you unearth the perfect item for them. It's a WIN/WIN scenario.

Work both sides of the business. If you find someone who has resort property for rent and you know people who want to rent it, approach the advertiser. Ask him if he would pay you a fixed amount of money for every customer you find for him. You'll be saving your friends from the hassle of finding a holiday resort and you'll be saving the advertiser from the hassle of screening potential tenants. You can collect a commission from both parties. To expand on this, source several properties for rent, charge the owners/landlords to list them on your web page, and charge a finder's fee. Then charge the renters for using your web page as a source. Everyone will be happy.

Warrior Byte

The Internet abounds with sites that welcome free ads. Advertising is *always* worthwhile, especially if it's free! If you're looking for something specific, the Internet contains the published versions of daily newspapers from all over the world. Ask people in newsgroups and chat rooms to find out if they know where that elusive treasure can be found. Here are a few sites to play around in:

Over four hundred sites where you can run free classified ads on the Internet:

http://www.uran.net/imall/FREE_Sites.html

Free classified ads can be posted at:

http://www.thenet-usa.com

All-Links helps you find all the newspapers online from everywhere in the wired world. Read 3,500 newspapers free, as well as access all the webchat pages and all the pages that help you use *Dynamic HTML* to design your own exciting web pages:

http://www.all-links.com

File Mine presents you with every type of software imaginable. Think how helpful that could be to the average computer user!

http://www.filemine.com

BOUNTY HUNTING

While you're out finding things, think about finding people. We've all fantasized about hunting down the bad guys and collecting a reward. It really does happen and not just on TV! Use the Internet to find out how to become a bounty hunter and then use the resources of the Internet to search for the information you need. You're no longer limited to your own locality—now you can search the planet for your prey!

Warrior Byte

Become a bounty hunter in three easy steps:

1. Learn how it's done.

You want to become a bounty hunter? Here's what you need to know to become a licensed bail bond person and get cash on delivery:

http://www.onworld.com/BHO

2. Find out who is missing and what it's worth to find them.

Who's wanted?:

http://www.ih2000.net/ira/ira.htm

3. Use some of the Internet resources to snoop around.

Warrior Byte

Hunting for someone? It's scary what the Internet can tell you:

**http://athos.rutgers.edu/~watrous/
people-hunting.html**

Find anyone through these directories:

http://www.att.com/directory/internet.html

In later chapters, you'll learn other techniques for finding people. The Warrior Bytes in this chapter provide you with some valuable starting points.

Remember: Knowledge + Innovation = Success.

CHAPTER SIX

HELPING OTHERS

■ ■ ■ ■ ■ ■ ■

> **Warrior Weapon**
>
> Don't forget to downsize the URL (*Uniform Resource Locator*) if a website turns up missing. Review the Warrior byte on page 44.

he best type of business to be in is one where you have the pleasure of helping others while earning money at the same time. This is called WIN/WIN. There is nothing more satisfying than doing something for someone else, but if doing something *to* someone else is more your style (i.e. revenge, retribution, vengeance...) the Internet can be your best friend. Either way, the Net is there to assist you in business or in monkey business.

No matter what your business, the Internet can provide you with the resources to improve your current status. If you are stuck in a rut, lacking the necessary new and dynamic ideas you need to attract clients, find out what works by seeing how it's done somewhere else in the world. Nearly every occupation and guild is represented by a website. Teachers can become better teachers by visiting sites that offer the latest child psychology and teaching techniques. Writers can become better writers by finding out what information sells and what markets demand. Craftsmen and tradesmen can improve their skills and surpass their competition with a little helpful advice from their Internet buddies.

People trying things for the first time can use the Internet to build confidence, to compete with others who have experience with a particular process. For example: are you planning to buy your first vehicle or purchase a fixer-upper as a starter home? What problems can you expect to encounter? The answers are out there. Consult the Internet first for an economical solution to every problem.

> **Warrior Byte**
>
> Before you buy that new or used car, you'd better get all the latest info at:
>
> **http://www.edmunds.com/**

Any help that you can provide through your Internet connection is invaluable to your friends and neighbors. If you have Internet access and they don't, think how much money you can save them by giving them the appropriate consumer report before they put their money on the line. Paying $20 to you to find out which item is the best buy prior to making a deal could save them hundreds in the long run.

There are countless ways that you can supplement your income using the Internet to assist acquaintances. The possibilities are mind-boggling. Start by helping your neighbor catch a cheating husband, then help her find a good lawyer!

Warrior Byte

Don't let life's little problems get you down. With the Internet, help is just a mouse click away.

So your husband came home with a strange phone number in his pocket... who could it belong to?

http://www.salesleadsusa.com/cgi-bin/abicgi/
abicgi.pl?BAS_session={bas_session}&BAS
_vendor+{bas_vendor}&BAS-type
=ADP&BAS_page=1&BAS
_action=search

Warrior Byte

Do you need a lawyer at home or abroad? Here's how you find one anywhere in the world:

**http://www.newquest.com/attorney/world/
worldsch.htm**

or

http://www.platinumpages.com/

How do you find a lawyer who will work for free (pro bono)?

**http://www.abanet.org/legalser/probono/
home.html**

as well as *Innovative Programs to Help People of Modest Means Obtain Legal Help in the US*

**http://www.abanet.org/legalserv/
modesthelp.html**

How do you know if the lawyer you've hired is any good?

http://www.nolo.com/nnmad.html

What about sweet Aunt Millie, who wants to leave $100,000 to charity? Help her find out what charities are legitimate. She should know if the money her favorite charity collects really goes to where it can do the most good.

Anyone who gives anything to any charity should consider the following:

- What is the organization's mission? What does it intend to do with the donations it receives? Are donations really used for their intended purpose?

- Do you know who leads the organization? Can you trust this person or persons to spend your money wisely?

- Does the organization give you access to its financial statements? Are your gifts and donations acknowledged? Is it a registered organization and are your donations tax deductible?

- Is the organization conducted in a professional manner? Are you assured of confidentiality and anonymity should you want it?

- Does the organization openly answer all your questions and concerns? Does it allow you to be deleted from its mailing lists should you wish?

The Internet can help you find out everything about an organization before you give them money.

> **Warrior Byte**
>
> *The National Charities Information Bureau* investigates the integrity of various charities to enable contributors to make informed choices. It attempts to provide accurate information and encourages people to support deserving and worthwhile causes. Improve your charities' performance by asking questions:
>
> **http://www.give.org/**

Perhaps your brother-in-law has been staying with you long enough to give you grey hair...how can you help him find a place of his own? Or it may be that your best friend has just gotten married and is moving a gazillion miles away. Help him and his new bride find a place to live before they get to their new destination (or before they change their minds and decide to move in with you and your brother-in-law...)

> **Warrior Byte**
>
> Help someone find a new place to live. There are over two million apartments to rent, all over the world, and they're all listed right here:
>
> **http://www.rentnet.com/**
>
> US apartments listed here, plus a map to tell you how to get to them:
>
> **http://www.allapartments.com/aa/**

The scope and breadth of the Internet is staggering. Once you get the hang of charging money for what you know, you'll find an overwhelming number of ways to earn money using your Internet skills.

HELPING OTHERS FIND MONEY OR SAVE MONEY

Warrior Byte

Businesses need a plan to get off the ground and a business or marketing plan is a required document when approaching a lending institution. Many websites offer helpful software for business and marketing plan development and for professional presentation:

http://www.brs-inc.com/

Don't overlook your federal government as an information resource. Do your research before applying for any business grant or loan:

**http://www.lib.uwaterloo.ca/discipline/
Government/CanGuide/Federal.html**

The Internet can help you do the necessary research to enable you to save money or find money for yourself or someone you know.

> **Warrior Byte**
>
> The Internet is a terrific resource when shopping for a loan—it allows you to do a multiple submission loan application, nationally. Fill out a form and receive a reply within twenty-four hours:
>
> **http://www.homeloansusa.com**

Find out if that new roofing company your brother hired is legitimate or fly-by-night by checking with your local Better Business Bureau prior to signing any contracts. A reputable company won't mind if you check references or investigate their background. There are on-line Better Business Bureaus for most major cities. The BBB can alert you to frauds and scams in your locality. You can also file a complaint immediately, so that other potential customers are alerted in time.

> **Warrior Byte**
>
> This website is provided by the *Council of Better Business Bureaus, Inc.* and the BBB system of over 150 Bureaus located throughout the United States and Canada:
>
> **http://www.bbb.org/**

There comes a time when someone you know needs money to start a business, write a book, go back to school or a hundred other reasons. The Internet is a great place to start your search for funds. In later chapters, there will be more specific information on how to find money for a particular pursuit, but you can always check out these Warrior Bytes. When you're applying for a specific loan, your presentation is important. It has to be professional and well thought out. Read the small print on each of these websites. Print out any documents so that you can read them on your own time (Remember, again, to DOWNLOAD information 'cause the meter's always running!) When you've gathered all the information you need, fill in your application and submit it.

Warrior Byte

Do you need a grant or a loan? Perhaps the *Federal Money Retriever Software* can help. This is one of many such programs available on the Internet. Do a search for *grant and loan software:*

http://www.idimagic.com/

Where can you find money for business or special projects on the Internet?

Corporate Grantmakers is a comprehensive site that lists private companies and foundations that provide funding. Definitely worth checking out:

http://fdncenter.org/grantmaker/corp.html

> **Warrior Byte**
>
> *Capital Quest* brings new business ideas to the attention of those who can help get it off the ground:
>
> **http://www.usbusiness.com/capquest/list.html**
>
> Non-profit organizations could try here:
>
> **http://www.capitalcampaigns.com/**
>
> *Microsoft* offers advice for *Canadian Small Businesses* on sources of venture capital, including how to write a professional business plan that will be the tool you require to approach a lender:
>
> **http://www.microsoft.com/canada/smallbiz**

Perhaps a small loan is all that's required. Your mission is to find a micro-loan. Micro-loans come from funds that are made available by non-profit sponsors. They provide money to entrepreneurs who probably would be rejected by their local bankers. Usually, the applicant is evaluated by a group of his peers who decide whether or not to approve his application. Those who approve an applicant's loan also become accountable for the debtor's performance. This provides an incentive for pay-back because no one really wants to disappoint a group of his or her peers.

Warrior Byte

If you or your client are having trouble arranging a loan, consider an alternative. *US Top Micro-Loan Lenders* are evaluated here:

http://tbzweb.com/lenders.htm

Be sure to downsize this URL for more business info!

Do you know a young adult or senior who wants to go back to school? Students are always looking for money to help them complete their education. Help them get that little boost they need:

Warrior Byte

Here's a comprehensive resource center that provides financial aid for students. Apply for federal student aid on-line:

http://www.finaid.org/

Fast Web helps students find sources of income fast:

http://web.fastweb.com/

Medical Student Assistance Fund:

http://www.ama-assm.org/med-sci/ erf/msasstf.htm

WORKING ON IT

There is no greater satisfaction than that which comes from making a difference in someone else's life. Provide an Internet service that does something truly worthwhile. Many people, young and old, are searching for work and many others are unhappy in their jobs. Why not provide a résumé service for these people? There are many computer programs that make creating résumés an easy task. Sit down with someone and help him or her put together a knock-em-dead résumé that will wow any prospective employer.

Warrior Byte

Here are some Internet sites that can help you create a résumé, even if you have no experience in this field whatsoever:

You can find sample résumés at:

http://www.eresumes.com

How to create a résumé and put it on-line:

http://titan.iwu.edu/%7Eccenter/resume/index.html

Everything you need to know about work including tips to help you get through the interview:

http://www.aboutwork.com/

If you choose to help other people find employment, you are doing a great service to your community. Gainful employment validates a human being and makes him feel he is contributing, doing his part, for his community. The individual, his/her family and the entire community benefit.

There are Internet sites to help you do a job search for every career imaginable. It would be virtually impossible to list all the places that introduce employees to employers. Your best bet would be to search for a specific type of job like *medical jobs, computer jobs, carpentry jobs*, etc... just type the word *employment* into any search engine and you'll come back with more hits than you can use in your lifetime.

Warrior Byte

Of course, you could charge for your time, but you can go a step further than most résumé services if you are connected to the Internet. For a fee of $10 per month, agree to submit a potential employee's résumé to as many potential employers as possible.

Where do you find these employers?

For job listings in major metropolitan areas:

http://www.careerpath.com

Warrior Byte

Connect the right person for the job with the right job for the person:

http://www.espan.com

This site bills itself as the nation's leading job resource:

http://www.jobtrak.com

Find over 50,000 jobs worldwide at:

http://www.monster.com

Canadian Jobs—Canada's answer to youth unemployment:

http://www.islandnet.com/~kmp/kmlinks.htm

Job Lynx boasts being the world's largest headhunter organization. (They do charge a small fee):

http://www.joblynx.com/joblynx.htm

It won't take you very long to discover a number of Internet sites that specialize in getting potential employees and employers together. Some services charge a fee but many are absolutely free. How many people do you think you could help by posting their curriculum vitae? Another WIN/WIN situation!

Another approach to job searching would be to join one of the worldwide trade associations in your area of expertise. They will help you gather information, develop your skills and network with other professionals in the industry.

Internet Newspapers are just as vital as the ones made from pulp paper. Newspapers contain want ads for a particular city or region. You can use software that will search for *Help Wanted* ads only. That weeds out a lot of unnecessary and time-consuming searches. Cover a lot more territory on the Internet in a fraction of the time you would spend wading through mountains of newsprint.

People willing to relocate will have an easy time finding work. The Northwest Territories and the Yukon in Canada, as well as Alaska in the United States, are crying out for workers in all trades and professions. Use the Internet to search the world for a job that's the perfect fit for a particular individual. Your unemployed clients should be encouraged to explore more than just their own locality. Some of the best jobs are located in rather remote areas. There is always work in the Yukon or Alaska. Even if a young person has no intention of settling into a northern community permanently, it's a good place to get work experience and earn a good dollar in a short period of time. As most have discovered, it's job experience that counts.

Here's how you can use the Internet to make money helping others search for work:

- Get tips to make the most exciting and professional-looking résumés.

- Post résumés for others at various Internet job boards.

- Collect job descriptions by location or by Industry and create a job database yourself.

- Create a list of job seekers and contact potential employers.

- Research companies for people who want to work there, giving potential employees an edge over other applicants when going in for an interview. This is called a backward employment search. In this case, you would source as much information as possible about a company that is of particular interest to a potential employee.

FRANCHISES

Many people dream of owning their own business. Purchasing a franchise offers several advantages over starting a business from scratch:

1. The parent company's name recognition is already in place and customers are pre-sold on the product.

2. Most franchises are *Turn-key* operations, meaning all support materials are provided prior to opening the doors

3. On-going support is provided from Head Office.

Using your Internet research skills, you'll be able to tell potential franchisees how much they can expect to pay for a particular franchise, inform them as to what is required of them and determine whether or not there have been prior problems with a particular franchisor by checking with Better Business Bureaus. Are other franchisees happy? Are they making money? Does the company support them?

Perhaps you know someone who owns an established business that has already built a terrific reputation. Provide them with the information they need to create their own family of franchisees and help them grow!

> **Warrior Byte**
>
> Help someone open up a franchise in your neighborhood:
>
> *Be the Boss* is a franchising website that will help you determine what business aligns with your talent and capabilities. Worldwide franchising information is provided:
>
> **http://www.betheboss.com/**
>
> If you already own a great business, how do you go about franchising it?
>
> **http://www7.homecom.com/host1295/**
>
> *Business Opportunities* provides a jumbo list of franchises:
>
> **http://www2.bizhotline.com/bizhotline/ classif/fran.htm**

> **Warrior Byte**
>
> *The Executives' Guide to Franchise Opportunities On-line* lists all the big franchises and a brief summary of their operations and franchisee requirements:
>
> **http://www.franchise-update.com/exec.htm**

GENEALOGY

One of the fundamental questions asked by mankind, individually and collectively, is "Where did I come from?" A need to *belong* is primal in us all. Just think how helpful the Internet can be in this search for our roots—having access to all the libraries in the world and obscure birth and historic documentation. People love to fantasize that they are descended from royalty, with entitlement to noble privilege. There are countless newsgroups and mailing lists devoted entirely to the subject of genealogy.

Genealogical researchers charge by the hour and find out such interesting things as a person's tartan or coat of arms, as well as their connection to celebrities, living or deceased. There is information readily available for tracking the lineage of almost any culture from Australian Aborigine to Zulu. The Internet broadens your information base to include any source worldwide.

When you research genealogy, you must consider that there many aspects to a search. Not only is the genealogy relevant, but culture and heritage as well. Census bureaus in most countries keep accurate records of the names, births and deaths of their citizenry. Cemeteries often contain valuable records that can be accessed on-line and you can find these by searching for *Census Bureau* or *Cemetery Records* for a particular county, city or country.

Family tree kits are available for a fee from many sources. These programs provide tutorials that are helpful in organizing your information as you gather it. Think of your search as a puzzle that you assemble piece by piece and do a search for *family tree software*. There are many libraries that specialize in genealogical research. Tracking family histories is a hobby that can become an obsession, particularly for elderly people who want to leave a historical legacy for their offspring. With a little innovation, a talent for research and a connection to the Internet you could become your local community's historian and genealogist.

Warrior Byte

Start your research at *Yahoo*, which lists hundreds of different societies and cultures. This provides you with places and people to contact:
http://www.yahoo.com

The Genealogical Research Library is also a good starting point:
http://www.grl.com

Another excellent resource is at *Cyndi's List of Genealogy Sites*, with more than 20,000 categorized and cross-referenced links:
http://www.oz.not/~cyndihow/sites.htm

TRAVEL

If people are always telling you where to go and how to get there; they are trying to tell you something. My advice is to stay exactly where you are and put your skills to work sending other people away!

It would be impossible to list all the sites that specialize in travel, but there are some ways you can make money searching through them. Unless you're a travel agent, don't bother searching for the cheapest fares or most convenient route to a specific destination and then booking the flight. Travel agents are already equipped for this and there are enough of them to go around, but you can offer your services as a *travel consultant*. Here are some ideas:

- Help people learn commonly-used foreign language phrases.

- Offer information on laws and customs of a particular area.

- Source Bed and Breakfast accommodation.

- Provide information on local campgrounds and recreational vehicle facilities.

- Provide a custom map of a city or phone numbers and locations of services they might need, like doctors, dentists and lawyers from the Internet Yellow Pages.

- Find out what's involved in purchasing a business or real estate in a foreign country.

- Find an Internet Service Provider so that people can conduct business and contact friends through E-mail while they're travelling abroad.

- Find out foreign currency rates and where to go to get the best exchange.

- Find out what assistance is available for disabled travellers.

- Offer advice on how to stay healthy in a particular country.

- Write about travel and what services you can provide in local newspapers and travel magazines.

Many of these services are covered in other chapters, but this gives you an idea of how helpful the Internet can be to anyone who is planning a business or recreational trip to another country. Any information that you can provide to make travelling a more comfortable and less stressful experience will be of value to tourists.

Warrior Byte

Book airline tickets, make hotel reservations, rent vehicles and more at this one-stop shop:

http://www.flifo.com/

This site boasts the lowest fares:

http://www.lowestfare.com/index4.html

Travel is an area where you can make many contacts through various newsgroups. There are people in virtually every country in the world willing to provide friendly, helpful advice. Contact fellow travellers who want to exchange their home for someone else's for a month, who would like to meet travellers from exotic cultures, or students who want to participate in foreign exchange programs.

Virtual travel guides offer visitors all the information they need to plan a trip without having to search many different sites. Check out travel guides for your clients to source accommodation, special events, tours, historical museums and points of interest. You can even use them to find out the projected weather forecasts. Many of these virtual travel guides provide complete, one-stop shopping, allowing you to rent a car, book a hotel room, find out about real estate and even locate a mechanic, if you need one. You can pay for everything in advance, using a credit card. Where do you find these virtual travel guides? Do a search for the country or city you are interested in and add the word *tourist*.

If you have friends or neighbors who can provide a service for tourists, convince them to set their business up on the Internet by joining a virtual travel mall. Do your friends run a bed-and breakfast or provide tour guide services? Do they make crafts, teach swimming or horseback riding? Customers visiting a virtual mall, armed with a credit card number, are prime targets for the astute business person. Advertise your business on the Internet and take full advantage of the impulsive buyer.

Warrior Byte

Here are some of the many sites that are helpful to tourists. Be sure to do an Internet search for a particular destination to discover the legion of resources that are available.

The List of all the Internet providers in the world:

http://thelist.internet.com/

This site contains advice and lists health services available to foreigners in various countries, as well as links for physically challenged travellers, including security tips. A good place to start:

http://www.casto.com/resource/health.cfm

Do you need to find a dentist in an unfamiliar city?:

http://www.dds.4u.com

What about finding a dentist in the middle of the night?

http://www.dentistinfo.com

What a service! Translate any language into any other language while remaining completely ignorant—or learn common phrases before you travel:

http://dictionaries.travlang.com

Travel scams and how to avoid them:

http://www.websciences.org/dvhpub/scams.htm

HEALTH RESOURCES

Good health is a fundamental element that dictates quality of life. Internet newsgroups are a precious source of information on almost any disease or cure in existence. Some of the information is so recent, your family doctor probably hasn't even heard of it. If your physician is open-minded, he will welcome the latest techniques suggested by patients and physicians from all over the world. If you have a particular interest in a specific disease, disability or treatment, it's imperative that you subscribe to all relevant mailing lists and newsgroups.

The Internet has great potential for good. Consider using your search skills for the sheer pleasure of helping humanity. Do you know someone who is ill with a chronic malady, for example? How can you alleviate their suffering? Do you know someone who has an intimate knowledge of a particular disease? How can their personal experience be used to benefit others?

Can you imagine how awful it must be to live with constant pain? Where can you get ideas for temporary pain relief techniques? Is there a way to control pain? Where can you find the latest information on pain relief? Wouldn't it be wonderful to have a conversation with people who have licked their pain problems? *Pain relief is as close as your mouse!*

In your search for answers to these questions, you'll be amazed at how helpful people can be. Your contacts will be worldwide, so you'll have the benefit of many diverse opinions and remedies. Organize all your knowledge into one helpful article, publish it and reach people who don't have an Internet connection—or put your article on a web page for all the world to benefit from.

Warrior Byte

For personal testimonials on various medical treatments, go to *DejaNews* and do a search for specific diseases. At this site you'll see news postings and the E-mail addresses of people who have various degrees of knowledge on these subjects. Once you have the names of some of the newsgroups where this particular disease is being discussed, switch to your news browser and post your questions or make your own contribution to that newsgroup:

http://www.dejanews.com/forms/dnq.html

PubMed provides free searches of the huge *Medline* database, formerly only accessible to physicians. Check it out at the *National Library of Medicine:*

http://igm.nlm.nih.gov/

Visit the *Pain Relief Reference Library* at:

http://www.arcticspray.com/as/html/ body_library.html

Here's how you can use your skills to help others and reap financial rewards at the same time:

- Offer to monitor newsgroups that specialize in a particular illness. Print out information.

- Subscribe to a mailing list pertaining to a particular disease. Print out information letters and send them to non-Internet users for a fee. Condense information and E-mail it to interested parties.

- Specialize in one particular area. If you know of a local seniors' lodge, for example, perhaps an arthritis newsletter would be helpful to the residents.

- Create a custom newspaper that contains the latest information on a specific disease.

- Collect recipes for special diets. There are excellent resources for diabetics, people with allergies and food-related illnesses.

- Deliver a powerful, inspirational message daily to subscribers' E-mail boxes. A positive, healing message is a great way to start the day.

- Create a web page that contains helpful information gleaned from various medical resources.

Warrior Byte

Medical Matrix is a free database that helps both medial professionals and patients alike. It covers so many topics and diseases that it is virtually impossible to list them all:

http://www.medmatrix/org/Index.asp

State Medicaid:

http://crossroads.gower.net/resources.html

An example of a personal web page that helps those who suffer from *Renal Cell Cancer* is at:

http://www.islandnet.com/~luree/cancer.htm

Create your own newspaper with subject matter that interests you:

http://www.crayon.net/

ANTI-AGING AND IMMORTALITY

While you're busy researching healthcare, pause for a moment at the fountain of youth…and bottle what you can for resale! We're living longer than ever before and thirst for knowledge that will provide us with optimal quality of life. This is the age of miracles. Use the Net to fish for anti-aging miracles worldwide—then distribute those miracles to a vast, hungry market that is willing to pay handsomely for whatever information you can provide. If you are already in a health-related business, supplement your supplements with valuable insights to ongoing health and well-being. A listing of some of the health-related fields include:

Plastic Surgery	Holistic Medicine	Laser Surgery
Vitamin Therapy	New Age Philosophy	Cryogenics
Exercise & Sports	Organic Gardening	Organ Replacement
Water Purification	Toxic Chemicals	Hormone Therapy

Anti-aging is a fledgling and untapped field that holds a special fascination for the baby boomer population. The Internet is the most diversified resource there is for information on current and historical facts on the subjects of health and mortality. Scientific knowledge is growing at a phenomenal rate. This is the first generation to taste the possibility of immortality and they want to know *everything!* Spread the word—cell rejuvenation is possible! According the *World Health Network,* we can expect to *double* our current statistical life span by the year 2040!

Warrior Byte

The World Health Network is interested in sharing the latest developments in anti-aging:

http://www.worldhealth.net

You'll find a whole website devoted to *Life Extension* right here:

http://student-www.uchicago.edu/users/ bmdelane/le.htm

The Eternal Life Device is believed to be the solution to aging and disease. You be the judge:

http://www.alexchiu.com/

FRIENDLY AFFILIATES

One of the least represented services that the Internet can provide is in the unusual area of friendly affiliates. This is where you provide a matchmaking service for a very specialized clientele. For example, there are many homosexual males who live in communities that are prejudiced about their sexual orientation. Gay males risk loss of jobs and personal safety if their true orientation is ever revealed to members of these communities.

There is a successful mail order service that matches males with compatible female partners for the distinct purpose of disguising the homosexuality of (in most cases) the male partner. The women get a secure living arrangement in exchange for housekeeping and being available for social functions. The males get to appear respectably straight in front of friends, family, employer or employees.

For a fee, you screen potential applicants to determine what they have to offer each other in order to form a mutually satisfying affiliation. This is a service that is desperately needed in nearly every urban area. So far, at the time of this writing, it only seems to be available in some German cities. Screening is the key to success in this operation. Your reputation depends on finding quality people who are well-matched and have mutually-beneficial objectives.

Screen all applicants carefully to ensure:

• There is sincerity and integrity on the part of both parties. A criminal reference check, as well as mental history would be recommended.

- There are some common outside interests, so that that both parties will enjoy attending functions together. Interests can include sports, hobbies, entertainment, fine arts and all other areas that constitute compatible union, other than, obviously, sexual compatibility.

- Make sure that each partner knows exactly what the other expects. There are many variables, such as one partner seeking financial support in exchange for housekeeping. There may be children involved, which is an important issue that needs to be addressed. Consider that these two adults will be entering into a contractual long-term relationship that is similar to a business arrangement, rather than a "love partnership" and skew your service accordingly.

- Protect yourself and your clients with appropriate legal forms. Get advice from a lawyer prior to embarking on this business venture.

Any special matchmaking service can be exceptionally rewarding, both financially and emotionally. Many of these unions last a lifetime. Hopefully, you will be instrumental in making two people happy—and the world certainly needs more happiness. You will also be charting new and unexplored Internet territory if you decide to open this service on-line.

A friendly affiliation is just one suggestion. There are many areas where your matchmaking skills can be helpful. People with disabilities need love, too, or at least a companion, in exchange for room and board. People need people. People need pets. Explore the potential field in your location and you'll come up with plenty of ideas.

CHAPTER SEVEN

IMPORT/EXPORT

■ ■ ■ ■ ■ ■ ■

> **Warrior Weapon**
>
> Mailing lists and bulletin board systems can be very helpful to your business. They are discussed on page 48.

The import/export business is one example of an operation that takes excellent advantage of the vastness of the Internet. The business skills required for this venture are applicable to any business you might choose to start up. Use your current knowledge to think globally instead of locally.

The Internet has much to offer new entrepreneurs in the exciting field of import/export, from advice, to markets, to brokers, to agents. Open up your mind and your market to broader possibilities, no longer limiting your thinking of your market to one designated area. The Net will instantly become the most valuable and well-rounded business partner you could ever have.

Warrior Byte

Need some good advice on starting a small business? Check here before you open up shop:

http://www.sb.gov.bc.ca/

Here's a Canadian site that means business!:

http://strategis.ic.gc.ca/

No matter what country you live in, there are local companies manufacturing goods that are saleable in another country... and there are foreign manufacturers who would love to break into your markets. If you're willing to put in the effort, you'll reap the rewards.

If you're serious about starting an import/export agency, you'll need a lot more information than I can give you here. Surf the web to learn about business management and the laws pertaining to your particular country. Consider the time you spend learning the business as time spent in *Real Life University*. Worthwhile knowledge is costly in time, money and effort, but you will gain valuable information that less resourceful people will gladly pay you for. This book will provide you with some Internet sites that can get you in touch with manufacturers, brokers and information providers. Arm yourself with as much information as possible before jumping into this or any business venture.

Remember to utilize newsgroups. *Usenet* is a type of network that facilitates communication among many people, much like a giant bulletin board, divided into specialized areas for people to post their personal news. Participate in Usenet newsgroups by downloading a free news reader like *Free Agent*. Usenet is teeming with topics like **alt.business.import-export** for just about any product imaginable. Usenet is a good starting point for gathering information and making contacts. Don't confine your Usenet search to import or export. Try monitoring groups that you find while searching for words like *broker* or *consult*. There are many *alt.business newsgroups* like **alt.business.offshore, alt.business.home** and **alt.business.franchise** that can provide you with ideas, testimonials and contacts. It wouldn't hurt to check out new *patents* while you're at it. You can never have too much data. Having access to current knowledge will give you an edge over your competition.

YOUR OWN INVENTION

So you or someone you know has invented the next paper clip and you know that everyone is going to need it. You'll want to know if it's been patented before. Use your researching skills to find out. Estimate charging $20 to $40 per hour for doing Internet searches for this information. In your search, you'll find manufacturers who may be willing to produce this new product by doing a search for domestic and foreign manufacturers. The secret to good searching is plugging in the right words. Try words like *exporter, distributor* and *broker.* There are so many places in the world crying to do business with you, that it would be foolish to limit yourself to the few addresses posted in this book.

> **Warrior Byte**
>
> Find out whether this new invention has been patented in the last twenty-six years by going to:
>
> **http://patent.womplex.Ibm.com**

Of course, conceptualizing a new product isn't all there is to it. You'll need venture capital to help in developing a prototype—or for ongoing manufacturing. You can always try the standard channels—begging from your friends and relatives, or your local banker. Now that you have Internet access, why restrict (or humiliate) yourself? Search out more unconventional, progressive and forward-thinking sources of support.

> **Warrior Byte**
>
> If you're looking for money to start up a new venture, there's lots of it available FREE! Check out sources US grants and loans at:
>
> **http://mel.lib.mi.us/social/SOC-grants.html**
>
> and Canadian grants and loans at:
>
> **http://www.island.net/~govprog/**
>
> If you're a whiz at filling out forms and talking the gibberish that government employees like to hear, you could earn a nice income helping others apply for the appropriate grants to get them started in their own businesses.

Your invention or idea is valuable to you. How can you protect it in the global marketplace? Some trade agreements like *NAFTA (North American Free Trade Agreement)* specifically provide protection for ideas. *The World Trade Organization* also provides a forum for settling disputes that arise over intellectual property.

> **Warrior Byte**
>
> Learn about International Trade from *NAFTA*. They want your business:
>
> **http://www.naftanet/it.htm**

If you plan to market your invention outside of your country of residence, you would be foolish not to ensure that you have the best protection possible. What may be protected federally may not be protected internationally.

COPYRIGHT

Any work, illustration, hard copy or hand-written copy that is your own original creation is automatically copyrighted by the use of the © symbol and the date. More than one hundred countries honor the *Universal Copyright Convention*, which recognizes this symbol. Protect yourself further from disputes of ownership by registering with the Copyright Office in your area.

TRADEMARK

If you conduct your business or sell your products using a distinguishing name, logo or symbol, you should register this trademark. To find out what the requirements are for your particular country or for foreign countries, contact your Patent and Trademark Office.

PATENTS

These give you exclusive rights over your invention or idea, but only for the country in which the patent was issued. There is a *Patent Cooperation Treaty* between several countries that allows you to register your invention or idea with the participating countries. Contact your Patent and Trademark Office for details.

While you're wading through all this information, it wouldn't hurt to make friends with a good trade attorney who specializes in international trade law. They can usually be found through your banker.

Warrior Byte

This site contains a wealth of links concerning copyright, trademark and patent law:
http://www.cais.com/iplaw/

United States Copyright Office:
http://lcweb.loc.gov/copyright/

Canadians can check out the information at *The Canadian Intellectual Property Office*:
http://strategis.ic.gc.ca/sc_mrksv/engdoc/cipo.html

UNDERSTANDING THE BUSINESS OF TRADE

Warrior Byte

Matchmaker Trade Delegations help small and medium-sized US companies establish business relationships in major markets abroad:

http:///www.ita.doc.gov/uscs/uscsmatc.html

Simply, when you're involved in the import/export business, you're bringing together buyers and sellers on a global scale. Whether trying to market your own invention or helping a company or individual market theirs, you must think globally instead of locally. You must constantly keep in mind that you're dealing with the import/export laws of your own country as well as the foreign laws pertaining to goods you intend to handle for your clients or yourself.

Here's where you must be a fearless warrior. Realize that international trade can be a complex business and it will require some effort on your part to unearth all the necessary and pertinent details. You'll have to be prepared to do considerable reading and on-going investigation, however, because very few people are prepared to make these "sacrifices", those who do will find themselves amply rewarded.

> **Warrior Byte**
>
> Import/Export trade information, with resource links all over the world:
>
> **http://www.importexporttrading.com/**
>
> *The Global Trade Centre* is a great place to get market information:
>
> **http://www.tradezone.com/welcome.html**

KNOW YOUR MARKETS

> **Warrior Byte**
>
> *The Trading Floor*, where exporters and importers meet in real time international trade exchange. Check out the action:
>
> **http://trading.wmw.com/**

The international trade markets are in constant flux. They depend on the political system that supports them. Each country has a different set of rules for what is allowed into and out of its borders. Find the most current information about the country with which you plan to trade through the Internet. With the Net infiltrating almost every country, trade barriers and restrictions are being forced down.

If you are just getting your feet wet in import/export, perhaps the easiest way to start is by being a sales agent. Sales agents find buyers and take a commission without worrying about shipping, documentation or financial matters. Once you have contacted a manufacturer, you must find a retailer to handle your product. Through the Internet, find the dates and locations of trade shows in your area where you'll be able to network with reps and distributors for your product. Search the Internet for trade associations and magazines pertaining to your particular industry. *It is advisable to run a credit check on anyone you plan to do business with.*

As an importer, you will have to know the tricks of getting items through customs. You must be cognizant of current tariffs and documentation requirements. All of the information required for each step of the process is available freely on the Internet, as well as in your local public library.

Exporting is a little different because you have to seek out foreign buyers for a domestic product. You'll be dealing with agents, state-controlled companies, or foreign distributors. The main resource for foreign buyers is your country's *Department of Trade and Commerce.* When utilizing this resource, the government performs all the credit checks for you. It's imperative that you learn everything you possibly can about screening clients before entering an export venture.

> **Warrior Byte**
>
> The *US Trade Center* helps Canadian and other foreign companies become successful exporters:
>
> **http://www.ustradecenter.com**
>
> *The International Trade Administration,* part of the US Department of Commerce, provides a number of free services to get foreigners started in exporting:
>
> **http://www.doc.gov/**

Perhaps the best trick in this business is to let the government do as much of the work for you as possible (and it *is* possible). Your Department of Commerce is very anxious for your business to succeed and bring more jobs to the community. Hopefully, you'll become a good source of tax revenue for them. The governments of trading countries can provide market surveys, contacts with agents and distributors and arrange appointments with key figures in the business. Furthermore, governments publish journals and bulletins containing the most current information on sources and contacts. Save yourself big consulting fees by seeing what your government has to offer first.

VENTURE CAPITAL

Choosing a bank that has experience in the import/export business is your first line of defense. If you are doing most of your trading with one country, look for a branch of their bank in your own country. Use a bank that is familiar with letters of credit and can handle many of the details for you. Your bank should be familiar with exchange currencies, transfer of foreign funds, import/export regulations and how to obtain credit information on foreign companies.

Ideally, you want more money coming into your business than going out of it. If you're a good money manager and have studied the market well, you're going to see a profit. There will be times when you may need additional funds to carry you through until payment is received for goods sold, where you have extended credit to a client who uses your services or purchases your goods. You may need money to expand you operations, hire employees, upgrade equipment or a myriad of other reasons. How can you get the necessary capital to conduct business?

(a) Short Term Loans

You should be able to demonstrate to your international bank that you have assessed your customer's credit risk and you have done your market research. You have written out your terms of credit so that the company you are dealing with knows exactly when and how much it has to pay. You have demonstrated a willingness to accept a cash discount for quick payment. Armed with this information, approach your banker.

The Overseas Private Investment Corporation

This US agency helps with financing and insurance. It's also a good source of direct loans to small businesses.

Warrior Byte

Overseas Private Investment Corporation is an independent US agency that assists companies interested in investing outside the country:

http://www.opic.gov

(b) Trade and Commerce

Don't overlook government sources, as your government actually encourages trade. Most governments know that foreign trade means local jobs. Be sure to inquire about which loans, grants or other assistance is available for your area.

(c) Your Suppliers

Some suppliers will let you purchase your start-up equipment on credit.

(d) Last Resorts

If you have been honest and reliable with your friends and relatives, you may be able to convince them that you are a good investment risk. You also might have equity in your home or personal property. Before you mortgage your progeny's college education, make sure that you've exhausted all other avenues.

WHAT YOU DON'T KNOW CAN KILL YOUR BUSINESS

Warrior Byte

The Export Legal Assistance Network could be vital to your survival:

http://www.miep.org/elan

Your major consideration, as with any business, is how you're going to be paid. You'll need to become familiar with some international collection methods. A lot of these methods are similar to those available in your country of residence, but because your debtors may be in foreign countries, collection could be considerably more complicated.

Warrior Byte

The Foreign Credit Insurance Association (FCIA) can help take the worry out of dealing with buyers who may default. (see *Eximbank* in SOURCES):

http://www.owens.com/insuring.html

Who needs it?

http://www.cei.org/bank.html

Besides collecting money, any good business person should stay on top of the following:

- **Proper Record-keeping and Bookkeeping**—If you're not sure what to do, your local Small Business Administration Office probably offers a course

- **A workable Business Plan**—Sometimes brainstorming with a consultant before you start anything new can save you lots of money and grief.

- **Taxes, Taxes, Taxes**—Make sure you fill out all the paperwork and comply with the law. It will catch up with you and potentially ruin you if you don't.

- **Advertising**—Learn what it takes to reach and stimulate your target market.

Warrior Byte

Not sure about the trade laws in your country or any other? Check it out at the *International Trade Law* site:

http://ananse.irv.uit.no/trade_law/nav/trade. html

This brief overview of the import/export business should give you some idea of what sorts of resources are available FREE on the Internet. Markets and currencies vary on a daily basis. By utilizing the most current information available, you'll be several jumps ahead of the competition, no matter what business you're involved in.

Warrior Byte

There are an incredible number of information resources on the Internet for any business, including the import/export business:

Export Central will help you get started in international trade:

http://www.exportcentral.com/

International Union of Commercial Agents and Brokers in Europe can help you make contacts:

http://www.netsource.fr/acx/

Trade Compass gives you the leads and tools you need for trading in international markets:

http://www.tradecompass.com/tools.html

THE STOCK MARKET

The import/export business is somewhat related to the stock market, so a brief mention here is warranted. There is so much information about the stock market on the Internet that, if you are interested in participating, you would be wise to buy one of the many excellent books on the market written on the subject. If you plan to do purchasing for other people, you must take the proper courses and apply for a license. Almost every major search engine has links to daily stock market reports. There are ample sites where you can make your purchases on-line. Brokers and bankers are willing to offer advice and set up accounts.

One area that deserves further investigation is specialized stock market analysis. Your experience with the Internet and computers will help you discover trading secrets that used to be available only to professionals. There are some excellent software programs to help you analyze and track market trends. These programs have made many investors wealthy. If you're thinking of opening a small investment club with a group of friends and neighbors, consider utilizing some of these expert programs. Few individuals have knowledge in this area, so your research will really pay off.

Warrior Byte

Titan Trading is a financial software development company that specializes in the research and analysis of stock market trading patterns. These programs are helpful when trading on world financial markets:

http://www.titantrading.com/

Here's an interesting site that allows you to do free research on various companies, manage your own stock portfolio and chat with other investors. They also run contests to give away stock shares. *Investment Hotlines*:

http://www.invhot.co

CHAPTER EIGHT

LOVE AND MARRIAGE

■ ■ ■ ■ ■ ■ ■

Warrior Weapon

If you are planning to send your photograph over the Internet, you might want to learn a bit about GIF and JPG, which were discussed briefly on page 62.

ant to "tie the knot" on the Net? First things first. You need to find the perfect partner… and your intentions must be in alignment with the needs of your true self. Some people marry because they're lonely, some marry for money, some because they want to start a family. Most of us are still incurable romantics and want to marry for love.

ON-LINE LOVE

Warrior Byte

Anyone can write to a *Cyberpal* at:

http://www.mbnet.mb.ca/crm/cyberpal

Are you tired of never getting any E-mail? Do you want to meet someone special for a serious romance or meet someone kinky for anonymous titillation—or just engage in some mutually stimulating conversation? Try *Web Personals* at:

http://www.webpersonals.com/

and

One And Only at:

http://www.one-and-only.com

for a modest fee you can *Click For Love*:

http://www.click4love.com

The Internet is an endless database for love. Do a quick search for Love and Marriage and you'll come up with over ten thousand websites. These are just the *general* places to start! If you're really serious about finding a mate you should be monitoring the newsgroups and chat sites as well.

In the alternative newgroups, refine your search to skew toward your particular interests. For example, by conducting a search for single, you'll find: *single.parents, single.christian, single.30plus, single.overweight* and more categories. Tweak your search to a hundred-mile radius by specifying a particular area. There are *aka.anchorage.singles* and *fl.tampa.singles*, as well as every other country on-line, each listing eligible people looking for a suitable mate.

The chat sites allow you to get as up-close and personal as your keyboard will let you. It's a step up from "letting your fingers do the walking". By talking with prospective mates on the Internet this way, you can get some idea of their likes, dislikes, interests and their sense of humor (or lack thereof). You can also send digital photos to each other so you have an idea of your dreamboat's physical appearance.

Most photograph developers nowadays give you the option of putting your pictures on disk. These can be converted to .GIF or .JPG format to send through your E-mail program and view in your browser.

A WORD OF CAUTION: As with all informal introductions, you must be very cautious. There are several horror stories about the wonderful cyber date turning out to be a stalker in real time. Or how about the Romeo who married several women in different states for fun and profit? How many guys have been enjoying an on-line romance with an Elle McPherson look-alike for several months, only to find out that they have been chatting with the male version? Oh well, nothing ventured, nothing gained. There are probably a lot more sincere and genuine people who are looking for love than there are deceivers and scoundrels. Don't let a bad experience discourage you from getting out there and having fun, but be very cautious about giving out too much personal information too soon.

Can you make money operating a matchmaking service on the Net? Definitely—if you specialize or handle it differently from anyone else. For example, localize your website to one small group or area. For $20 a year, list someone's advertisement on the Internet at a site that specializes in students only from a particular college...or a site that helps people with handicaps make contact with others with disabilities...or a site that unites people with a particular hobby, like skin-diving or mountain climbing.

How do you reach those who don't have Internet access? For a monthly fee, you can print out and mail ads that would provide a broader contact area than what is reached in the local newspaper. Answer ads for these people and post their ads for them. Speaking of newspapers, don't forget that the Internet has access to every newspaper, everywhere, at the click of a mouse. Provide your customers with personal ads from any country they happen to be interested in. If they are seeking a Japanese pen-pal or a Swedish lover, you have the capacity to bring the contact ads directly to them.

If you're an accomplished wordsmith yourself, provide a letter-writing or poetry-writing service for those who are too shy or lack the skills to come up with the words they need to woo their particular love interest. Come up with ten or so letters of introduction that can be used to pique the interest of advertisers. Change these letters slightly to fit each situation and you've got yourself an answering service for the lovelorn.

Here's a sample letter:

Dear (insert name or advertisement number):

Your advertisement was most exciting to me because I share similar interests and values to your own. I am (give a physical description, age, general appearance, or whatever information your client wants to reveal). My interests include (list hobbies and pastimes that your client finds enjoyable—sports, fine dining, watching television... you might also want to include information such as your client's education and employment, or if they have any children). Like you, I would like to meet someone who (list some common ground—e.g. wants to start a family, wants to be friends first, wants to meet someone who has high moral standards).

Could we meet over coffee to discuss mutual interests? (Make the meeting as non-threatening as possible and always in neutral territory, like a coffee shop or restaurant. Be sure the advertiser feels no pressure or obligation by accepting this invitation). I look forward to making your acquaintance.

Sincerely,

Name:

Address:

Phone Number: (can they call collect?)

If the advertiser lives far away from your client, it is a courtesy to include a stamped, self-addressed envelope for their convenience. The odds of receiving a response are much greater this way.

It feels good when you're instrumental in putting lonely people together. If you can make money making people happy in this way, you're enjoying one of the greatest benefits of free enterprise.

ON-LINE MARRIAGE

Ain't love grand? It's definitely one of the most powerful forces in our universe. It makes you want to do things for those you love. It makes you want to morph from a party animal to a decent human being. It brings out the best in all of us—compassion, hope, nurturing, tenderness. When cupid strikes, we want to get married.

Help those who want to get married, but don't want all the hassle of those annoying trappings, like renting a hall, buying food for relatives they've never met (or never want to meet), paying big money to bands, caterers, dressmakers, ad infinitum. Here's your opportunity to provide economical wedding coordination services or actual wedding services on the Net! There are all kinds of different wedding services around, but many people are looking for something a little out of the ordinary. Cyber Marriages are unique, quick and easy... and economical.

Warrior Byte

Gain instant respect and perform legal marriages by becoming ordained on-line at *Universal Life Church*. Get even more respect by becoming a Doctor of Metaphysics or Doctor of Divinity while you're at it:

http://ulc.org/ulc/

The law is constantly evolving where marital legislation is concerned and all current statutes are published on the Internet. What is required for a legal marriage?

1. The intent to get married must be publicized by purchasing a license or having banns published in church. (Banns are proclamations stating where the marriage will be taking place so that people have an opportunity to object to the union).

2. A properly ordained official of a permanently established religious body, or a licensed marriage commissioner, must perform the ceremony.

3. The two people being married must be present. No one can stand in as a replacement for either party.

4. The marriage must be witnessed by at least two other people.

5. The parties must affirm that they are legally qualified to get married (i.e. they are not already married to someone else and they are not blood relatives).

6. There must be a formal pronouncement that the couple has become husband and wife.

7. A statement of marriage must be filled out and signed by the couple, as well as the witnesses and the ordained minister, who usually presents them with this paper. The document must be registered with the proper authority (the state or province where the minister carried out the ceremony).

With the invention of Internet cameras, the two parties don't have to be in the same country to participate in the ceremony. Being "present" at a Cyber Wedding can mean *by photographic image only.* There are programs that also allow you to send your signatures over the Internet. As the person performing the marriage, you must check the age restrictions and any other limitations imposed by the state in which the marriage ceremony is being performed. Some places do not allow homosexual marriages, but if you run your Internet marriage service from a state that does, the marriage will be recognized, even if the participating parties don't live in the same state.

Are these marriages legally binding? The marriage must be recognized in the jurisdiction in which it takes place. In most cases, even if someone who was not properly authorized to do so conducted the marriage, it still remains valid. If the ceremony was carried out in good faith and was intended to be in compliance with the law, the couple is legally married. The one provision is that they must live together as husband and wife after the ceremony (an unconsummated marriage is grounds for annulment in most states). To find out what laws apply in your state or province, check with the appropriate authorities.

ON-LINE DIVORCE

Getting out of love's tender trap can be a lot more difficult than getting into it. The flight for freedom is never easy and people need very specific advice in these situations. When children are involved, it becomes even more complicated.

If you're a lawyer, you might be able to attract some clients to your business by setting up a helpful advice page. However, performing on-line divorces is nowhere as neat or simple as on-line dating or on-line marriage. Uncontested, no-fault (or "quickie") divorces can be performed on-line if there are no complications. Even then, the laws of your state or province would determine any restrictions. This is one moneymaking scheme that would require further in-depth research prior to opening up shop.

Warrior Byte

Divorce Resources—Need to know how to file your own divorce or where to find a good attorney?

http://www.iimagers.com/divorce-resources.html

ON-LINE ADOPTION

You've found your soul mate and now you want to make your life complete with a family. What could be more gratifying than giving a home to a child who doesn't have one? This is a major long-term commitment that requires many sacrifices—don't make this decision lightly or without a great deal of soul-searching and serious research. Take your time with this—there can be far-reaching ramifications if things don't work out and people's lives can be destroyed in the process.

Foreign adoptions may appeal to you, especially if you are having difficulty obtaining a child locally. Unfortunately, foreign adoptions are teeming with hazards. Perhaps one of the best ways to get first-hand information is to search the Usenet groups for the word *adopt*. You will find an abundance of listings under *alt.adopt*, from *alt.adopt.latvian.babies* to *alt.adoption.problems*. Join one of the many adoption newsgroups on the Internet where you can discuss your concerns and desires with other parents who have paved the way. Remember: on the Internet, you're not alone. There's always someone as near as your mouse to offer good advice to prospective parents. If your dream is to adopt children, go for it! As any good warrior, always arm yourself with the best information possible.

You can help others over adoption hurdles. Using the Internet, provide valuable information to those who want to know all the details prior to adopting. What kind of child are they looking for? Will they accept a child of a different race? What about a child that is emotionally, intellectually or physically challenged? Where should they go and who should they talk to? The preliminary information you can provide may be vital to their making a decision that will affect the rest of their lives…and the lives of any prospective adopted children.

> **Warrior Byte**
>
> Prospective parents need a reliable information source on adoption:
>
> **http://www.adopting.org/**

CHAPTER NINE

THE WRITE STUFF

■ ■ ■ ■ ■ ■ ■

ooks abound on the subject of writing and where to sell it. If you're reading this book, you're probably more of a realist than a novelist and starving while you write is less appealing to you than making money from what you write. The Internet is full of facts and data just waiting to be molded into saleable stories and articles.

Ever since people discovered the power and magic of language, they've wanted to play with it. The Internet has turned into the greatest open forum in history for writers all over the world to share and display their words. Writing that excites and inspires is the writing that gets attention. It's often controversial and always stimulating. Don't be afraid to offend anyone. Express yourself—share your ideas—*write like a warrior!*

EXPANDING YOUR MARKETS

Warrior Byte

Writing resources:

http://pages.prodigy.com/MN/qgrv70b/wrtg-top10.html

Market it, publish it, sell it! *The Electronic Newsstand* lists over 2,000 magazines to help you zero in on potential markets:

http://www.e-news.com/home/

Don't forget the electronic magazine market:

http://www.wolfe.net/~lbothell/3slinks.htm

While you're dreaming about finishing the greatest story ever told, you have to realistically examine the markets that are buying writing. Start by selling information to individuals while you gain confidence and skill. It's hard to make a decent buck selling information to individuals, so you'll need to begin thinking expansively.

Let's say you're gathering information to produce one speciality item for one consumer. Whatever information you've gathered for one consumer can be recycled and re-used for a wider audience. Don't let all the research go to waste! A report on Mexican Health Care, produced for one client, could grow into a report on the Joy of Using Mexican Pharmacies or the Perils of Mexican Diseases, which could be sold for travel brochures or small magazines.

Always look for a broader market, or any way to slant your story, making it saleable elsewhere. Examine the pros and cons of every situation so that you can sell to adherents on both sides of the fence. Remember: *Warriors are irrepressible opportunists!*

Here's an example of expansive thinking: Perhaps you've been commissioned by a local parents' group to gather information on Christian Colleges so that they can make an informed decision about the best ones to send their children to. Where can this information be marketed?

1. Christian magazines and newsletters would be interested in a report about the ratings of various colleges. They might also be interested in topics like campus activities, extracurricular sports, co-ed dating, safety, health and other features of college life. If your research includes this information, it could be fodder for a separate article.

2. Be an equal-opportunity writer. Sell this same information to a non-Christian market with a slant on secular schools.

3. Perhaps a Catholic magazine might be interested in *Schools Named After Famous Saints.* Discuss the merits of each of the schools listed.

4. Get your warrior adrenaline flowing by writing an article for secular papers that examines the argument *Do Christian Colleges Provide a Superior (or Interior) Education to Their Students?*

5. The general public might thoroughly enjoy an article asking *Should Our Taxes Be Supporting Religious Education?*

6. Women are important people too, at least in some parts of the Western Hemisphere. Parents might wonder *Are Patriarchal Colleges Harmful to Female Self Esteem?*

7. Don't stop now! What about providing information on *Campuses that are Friendly to Minority* (Black, Hispanic, Muslim, etc.) *Students.*

8. And maybe, just maybe...*Christian Campuses that Allow Pets.*

A true warrior lives by his/her wits. Every piece of individual research that you do should generate at least five other potential markets. Never stop thinking. *If you let your brain die, you might as well join it!*

MAKING HARD COPY

If you can read and put together a decent sentence, you have all you need to start making money. Begin with your local newspaper. Small papers are looking for amusing filler articles that tell a humorous story or explain the origins of a saying or a game or philosophy. There is an abundance of this sort of information the Internet.

As you gain confidence and discover your forte, write full-length articles about local history, or how-to, or interview residents in your community. If you have web page-building skills, offer to put your local paper on-line.

Warrior Byte

The news just keeps getting weirder and weirder:

http://www.newsoftheweird.com/

Everyone could use a laugh:

http://www.intermarket.net/laughweb/

History, gleaned from the Internet, can also be printed on paper place mats which can be sold to restaurants in your community. For additional income, sell advertising space on these place mats. People who sit in restaurants are virtually a captive audience.

Laminate the place mats and sell them to tourists and residents alike or use them to raise money for a school or town museum, with proceeds being split between you and the recipient.

Using similar methods, put together a community cookbook or a collection of animal-treat recipes for your local Human Society. There are countless recipes of every description available (for anyone's use) on the Net. Make sure the recipes you choose aren't copyrighted. Most are not, so if you encounter a site whose owner claims are copyrighted, move on to a friendlier site.

The Internet is full of non-copyrighted material that you can rephrase and use to create your own articles, newsletters, pamphlets, place mats or whatever printed materials you can conjure up. There are jokes for every occasion, to help your neighbor write that speech for his brother's wedding. There are fortunes and misfortunes, horoscopes and horrorscopes. There are epitaphs, anecdotes and news items that only need your creative talents to be collated into a useable format. Can you help someone by writing a memorial service, creating a special valentine, writing a letter to the editor or a complaint to a local business? Could your community use a monthly newsletter that lists all the coming events, while featuring some local gossip, humor, business profiles or all of the above? Each piece of information you need to gather is right there on the Internet. If you've read Chapter Three, you already know how to get it.

INFORMATION BROKER

Warrior Byte

There's no need to pay for information. *Virtual Reference Sites* contain over 2,500 of the most popular information reference sources on the Web. Things like calculators, dictionaries, directories, zip codes, maps, languages, free stuff, jobs, weather, travel, white & yellow pages, health, humor, etc., etc., etc... from "Art" to "Youth" and everything in between.

**http://www.dreamscape.com/frankvad/
reference-business.html**

Using the Internet for all your research, you can compile an incredible amount of information for anyone who wants to use your services. In fact, information brokerage businesses are really hot right now. Your start-up costs are your computer, printer and Internet connection.

Most businesses and government agencies can't afford the time or manpower that it takes to gather specific information. Many man-hours are required to collect the pertinent information, read it, catalogue it and organize it into a useable format. Information brokers are needed to perform all these tasks.

Find out what sort of information is needed by your local offices. Do they need to know how many people can be expected to purchase new houses in the area? Do they need to know what kind of wildlife is endangered before issuing hunting licenses? Do they need someone who can access information databases on a freelance basis?

Warrior Byte

There is a huge database maintained for legal professionals as well as business and journalism experts. This database amounts to the equivalent of piling CD-ROMs to the height of a seventeen-story building:

http://www.lexis-nexis.com

SPECIALITY SHEETS

There is a tremendous need for specialized information and you can make a reasonable income by providing answers to the local citizenry. All you need is a computer, an Internet connection and a printer. A small advertisement in seniors' magazines, local newspapers or trade magazines could read something like this: *'The Answer Man will find out information on any topic. $5 and up.'*

Here are a few examples of what your information service can provide:

1. Recipes for special diets. This could include cooking for invalids, diabetics, gluten-free, vegan, etc. The list is endless.

2. Travel information for any destination, currency exchange, safety tips, customs and manners.

3. A fact sheet of real estate costs for any country. Risks, complications and things for purchasers to consider.

4. Lists of lawyers, doctors, accountants, specialists, or contacts for any country in the world.

5. The latest information on any disease, make-up techniques for cancer patients, exercises for arthritis sufferers.

6. Research for student essays or theses. Scientific, literary and historical research.

7. Special projects for clubs, science fairs, Boy Scouts, etc.

8. Street maps for almost any major city.

9. Hair styles for bad-hair days, unique patterns for quilts and woodwork, plans or speciality items, from how to build your own still to how to raise happy earthworms.

Warrior Byte

Travel can be a blast with your own personal map from:

http://www.mapblast.com

Show up on the doorstep of your favorite business:

http://www.zip2.com

Worldwide Maps to local streets right here:

http://www.argusmap.com/

Ideas for information providers would fill an entire book Use your imagination. Ask yourself *"What information would I like to know?"* Look in speciality magazines that cater to a specific age group, economic status or trade and ask *"What sort of things are these people interested in? What information could I provide to help them with their hobbies, concerns or professional development?"* Once you've acquired a reputation for providing timely research at a reasonable price, your business will grow rapidly.

COMPANY NEWSLETTERS

Every business can promote itself by publishing its own newsletter. The letter can appear on the Internet as a web page, can be E-mailed to subscribers and a hard copy made for regular snail mail.

Remember that a newsletter is exactly that—a newsletter. It's primarily an industry newsletter, even though it may contain advertising. It's not an advertising or sales brochure. Give the readers some interesting facts about the company and its products and slant any news articles to show your client's products in a favorable light.

If you're not too sure how to start a newsletter, follow the format of a regular newspaper. They have eye-catching titles that entice readers to read the articles. Use pictures and color to grab their attention. Build your own reference file of newsletters for on-going ideas.

Approach local businesses initially. Develop a quality product and you will attract a larger clientele.

Warrior Byte

Learn how to do great company newsletters:

http://www.companynewsletters.com/ newsread.htm

VANITY PUBLISHING

Warrior Byte

Get help honing your writing skills:

http://www.inkspot.com/

People are vain. Anything that you publish about a local individual can also be published for the whole world to see on the Internet. Contact families who have lost a loved one to see if they would like a memorial website erected. Contact local Scouts, Girl Guides, community sports teams, etc. and spur their interest in publishing their accomplishments for the entire world to read. Local parents would love to see their children's best stories, poetry and artwork tastefully displayed—something that would become an academic incentive for otherwise reluctant learners.

A comfortable income can be made by publishing books that review local websites. Of course, all the web page authors want copies of the books for family and friends. It's very easy to find web pages for your community, just by looking at any ISP home page, where their customers' pages are listed. After you compile your reviews, notify web page owners by E-mail and tell them that their site is critiqued in your book. Allow them to pre-order at a special rate.

Along the same vein as vanity publishing is the production of specialized newspapers. Compile information for a newspaper containing all the exciting events that happened on someone's birthday. Simply do a search specifying the date you want to research. Using a newspaper story format, proclaim the accomplishments and attributes of the birthday person. Pet owners love documents for their favorite pets, listing achievements, pedigree or unique characteristics. These types of specialized newspapers could be laminated and framed as momentos of a child's birth, graduation, anniversary or any one of a number of distinguished occasions. For a list of prospective buyers, peruse the announcement section of your local newspaper.

While you're in the business of creating specialized newspapers, why not gather all the information you can on a specific celebrity? This can be compiled into a one-of-a-kind newspaper for the birthday girl or boy. How many teenage girls would love a paper containing all the Leonardo you can stand? What about little-known Kennedy facts? Or all the Elvis sightings in the world? Whatever information you pull together, there's a market for it.

Warrior Byte
Do you want to publish your own book? Here's a site for sore eyes:
http://www.pma-online.org

WARRIOR WRITING (AKA FLEECING THE SHEEP)

It's incredible what people will believe! You'd almost think they *want* to be fooled! Maybe it's in our genes. When you live in a boring neighborhood with boring friends and work at a mind-numbing job, you're entitled to a little mental stimulation. What could be less boring than to believe that something fantastic is happening around you? Or to believe in *free money?!*

> **Warrior Byte**
>
> Could you use $1,112,000? This prize is available to anyone who can actually demonstrate something supernatural. They must be prepared to allow scientific scrutiny of their claim.
>
> **http://www.randi.org/jr/**

There is also the distinct possibility that the general population is too lazy to do any serious investigation on any subject. It's definitely much easier to sit in one place and absorb information from the television, radio, newspaper or local guru. If you expect to help others and yourself through the use of your writing skills, you'd better arm yourself with knowledge. People would rather come to you for advice and pay for the information than do the research themselves. Use the various web resources that appear throughout this book to do a thorough check on any business before you (or anyone you know) put your hard-earned pennies on the line. Your ability to use the Internet to do research (which nobody else has the "time" or inclination to do) will pay off handsomely.

> **Warrior Byte**
>
> It's absolutely unbelievable the number of cons, frauds and hoaxes that are perpetrated on the unsuspecting public every day. See for yourself:
>
> **http://www.andrew.cmu.edu/user/td2b/ conmen.html**
>
> If you really expect to make money fast, you'd better check here first:
>
> **http://user.me.net/~miketoth/scam.html**

For every hoax that is perpetrated, there are die-hard believers. A recent example of spurious reporting occurred with the television documentary on the discovery of Noah's Ark., which was later proven to be a hoax. In fact, Richard A. Fox won an award for his magazine article that analyzed the program and questioned the authenticity of the story. The article was entitled *The Incredible Discovery of Noah's Ark: An Archaeological Quest?* It appeared in the Summer 1993 issue of *Free Inquiry*. His article was also given national attention in *Time Magazine*. Very few people seem to remember Fox's article but there are plenty of people who think that Noah's Ark has been found.

What about that notorious *Alien Autopsy*, which garnered its own television show? The audience was asked to form their own opinions about authenticity and there was never any objective, scientific proof presented, but how many people believe that the detailed dissection of an alien creature was depicted?

> **Warrior Byte**
>
> Aliens: are you a believer?:
>
> **http://www.newageinfo.com/res/ufo.htm**
>
> or a skeptic?:
>
> **http://www.csicop.org/articles/2020/**

There is an excess of Internet sites claiming to hold the secret of paying no income taxes (for a fee, of course). If you set yourself up as a *Private Sovereign Entity*, you are not regulated by US law and, theoretically, not liable for taxation. Unfortunately, there is no such thing as a private sovereign entity. Those that claim this is part of the 14th amendment are in for a rude awakening. Tax laws are applicable to all people in the United states, even foreigners working in the US.

The population at large has a tendency to minimize the factual and dwell on the fantastic—and that's a fact! Never over-estimate the intelligence of the human race. We all need, however, to justify our beliefs—at least to ourselves. We want to be able to present a reasonable argument when questioned about our convictions.

Knowing this and being armed with an effective presentation, we are able to make many people believe almost anything.

> **Warrior Byte**
>
> Protect yourself from Internet frauds and scams. *The National Fraud Information Center* is one of the best resources for checking out any business schemes:
>
> **http://www.fraud.org/**

CREATING FACTS

How do you make a story appear credible?

1. Interview someone who thought they actually saw something.

2. Interview a friend of someone who thought they saw something. This will provide witness corroboration. It doesn't matter if they were actually present during the occurrence of the event.

3. Build up a base of credibility for the witness. For example, state the witness was a local virgin. Virgins are pure, ergo they wouldn't fabricate an event. Or interview a local sheriff. Sheriffs are respected members of the community, so they must be telling the truth. Your story immediately gains more points on the believability scale than it

would if your witness was a topless dancer or someone facing a traffic violation. If the only witness was a topless dancer, focus on her being a hard-working University student. If the witness was the town drunk, promote him as a devoted family man. Skew the facts in your favor.

4. Take pictures of people or objects that have some relation to the story. Even if the photos have nothing to do with any factual evidence, pictures always promote credibility. Take a picture of the rock where the aliens landed. Take a picture of the dog who was scared by a ghost. Take a picture of the uncle of the boy whose sister saw the blessed saint at the local disco. If the story is illustrated with a genuine photograph, it must be true!

Does this stuff work? Examine a classic case from the Bible:

1. John says a woman named Mary went into a tomb and didn't see anything. Off she went to recount what she didn't see.

2. Matt says two women named Mary went into a tomb where they saw an angel and then ran to tell everyone what they had seen.

3. Mark declares that it was Mary, Mary and Salome who went into a tomb and saw a young man. One of the women named Mary ran out to try and get people to believe the story. Mark later changes his tale to say that the women didn't say anything to anybody because they were too afraid.

4. Luke then tells everybody that a whole bunch of people went into a tomb and saw two men.

5. None of these men—John, Matt, Mark or Luke were actually in the tomb themselves in order to witness anyone else seeing anything.

(See the SOURCES section for the exact words to this story).

Whether you believe the story or not is irrelevant. The point is, people are still making lots of money from telling it. There are whole industries built around it, as there are with UFO's, psychic phenomena, Elvis sightings and many other quasi-possible occurrences.

How do unscrupulous people make money from simply knowing that people will believe anything? First of all, they have to promise to deliver something in exchange for other people's money. Whether they can actually deliver on the promise is really of no consequence. People have to believe in the promise before they'll hand over their money. They want to believe they're getting terrific value for their dollar. Once they've paid, they'll seldom admit that there is the possibility that they could have been mistaken. Very few people ask for their money back when told the truth about an event.

Promise that the aliens left a message of health and immortality for believers. What's in the message? Buy the article to find out. How many people have the courage to admit they are wrong or were duped? They'd rather pay up and shut up.

Warrior Byte

Establish yourself as a US government 501c3 Tax-exempt organization by incorporating as a "Church". Gain the freedom to use your money in more constructive ways than the ways in which the politicrats would use it. To be officially recognized as a non-profit, tax-exempt church, your organization will have to file Form 1023 - *Application for Recognition of Exemption under Section 501(c) (3) of the Internal Revenue Code*. Let this Baptist website show you how:

http://www.helwys.com/fncinfo.htm

ENTERTAINMENT ENTERPRISE

Many Internet businesses operate *for entertainment purposes only*. Consider how a psychic hot-line works and then ask yourself if you could produce a daily individual E-mail horoscope for clients and charge them an annual fee for it. Psychics are able to provide people with astounding insights, which positively amaze their customers. Some intuitive wisdom includes:

"Even though you appear outwardly content, there is some internal pain." (Never specify whether it is physical or emotional suffering. This plays on the likelihood that everyone has something that bothers them).

"Someone close to you, perhaps a family member, is experiencing problems."

We all know someone who is sick, has financial difficulties or is in a troubled relationship.

"No matter what you do, you never quite attain the goal you want." (Isn't this the truth!)

Get the picture? The common thread with psychic babble is that clients must be convinced a psychic is their only source of insight—only a psychic can see clearly their unique, one-of-a-kind problems. People send money to psychics to have them encapsulate their personal problems for them, allowing them to determine their own solutions. They would probably achieve the same end result with a good psychologist.

An unfortunate sideline to the psychic business is the passport business. When someone gives their name and date of birth to a psychic, they run the risk of having their identification used for other than astrological purposes. Be on the lookout for psychics who ask personal questions before giving you information. Does a psychic really need to know your mother's maiden name?

There are some legitimate, tax-paying psychic businesses in operation. The point is, where there is a need, there is a way to make money filling that need.

There are similar businesses that do not pay taxes and prey on people by filling them with guilt and a sense of obligation. Let's examine the business practices of a typical Evangelist, using some representative mail solicitation. (See SOURCES in order to obtain samples of Evangelical literature).

1. Step one is to take a good guess at what your client's problem is. "Is this happening to you? I see a medical condition that sometimes causes weakness and pain. Is this happening to you? I see someone trying to hurt you and upset your peace. Is this happening to you? I see a deep desire for business success but something always holds you back."

2. Say to your customer something like "It's two in the morning and I have been on my knees praying for you." Personalize any computer-generated mail you send to your potential customer. This makes it seem more sincere and creates some type of bond between you.

3. Make your potential victim feel guiltier by sending them a little gift, like a prayer handkerchief. Give them explicit instructions because people feel more in control of their lives when they do something specific. "God has asked me to tell you to do this…exactly. Write down the one thing you really need on this prayer handkerchief and send it back to me with an offering of $50." (Note: there is no *fee* for this service—only a specified *donation*.) "Expect to receive God's blessing of a mighty financial miracle."

4. Keep on begging, "I know you may have to take this from your savings or from some other source…but remember, I am God's servant on earth and am here as a messenger on His behalf."

5. Threaten them with the loss of God's blessings. "You must not, in God's name, put this letter away. It is imperative that you obey the Will of God. Your gift, to help this ministry, will have an impact on the Heart of God."

6. Keep them coming back. If the expected miracle doesn't happen, they should send more money, to enable you to pray harder for them.

As you have surmised, there are not that many differences in creating psychological dependency in your clients, no matter what entertainment business you're in. The main difference is that some businesses are exempt from paying the taxes we all have to pay because they are doing *God's work.*

If you have ever been in business for yourself, you are probably fully aware of all the little annoyances your government inflicts on business people. Besides all the taxes and paperwork, your business must give fair value and deliver on its promises. There is the Department of Consumer Affairs to answer to. Furthermore, unsatisfied customers can launch a complaint with the Better Business Bureau if they are unhappy with your service. You are not allowed to gouge the public with excessively high prices. You are accountable to the government and the tax department. If you claim that you can cure someone or can get someone into heaven, you'd better be able to do it! Right now you're probably asking yourself, "Why should I give a third to half of my earnings to a government that doesn't demand *anything* from some guy who is selling $50 handkerchiefs?"

Why doesn't your local politician stop outright fraud and charlatanism? Surely your elected representatives must realize that, if they taxed all businesses (even the religious), revenues could be used to build clinics that would help the sick and the elderly much more effectively than prayer handkerchiefs? The money could be used to build community centers with outreach workers, to help lonely pensioners. Shouldn't a more tangible, proactive approach be taken to curing loneliness and disease?

Politicians are the ultimate psychologists. They have studied human nature in order to gain the votes they need to stay in power. Politicians realize that:

1. The average voter is basically primitive, superstitious and too lazy to do any investigation for themselves to uncover truth. People won't even read the HELP section that comes with most computer programs. How likely is it that the average person will go to a library or contact a professional consultant in order to obtain real and lasting solutions to their problems?

2. The average voter is totally gullible. Most people would rather believe anything than take responsibility themselves. Most people lack the confidence to believe that they are capable of doing good things on their own, without guidance.

3. The average voter will give their vote and their money to anyone who can offer a quick fix. Long-term planning and foresight aren't part of the

average person's character. People want a quick fix—they don't want to be accountable and would rather have someone else make decisions for them. That way, there's always someone else to blame when things go wrong.

This may seem like a harsh generalization, but it works to the advantage of the typical politician, who is also only human (honestly), with his own insecurities and fears. How many voters bother to investigate bills that have been passed while their representative was in power? The occasional hotshot news reporter can sometimes uncover a crafty scheme, but on the whole, a shrewd politician can get away with almost anything, from raising his own salary to giving favorite businesses special concessions. It happens every day in governments everywhere.

Sadly, there are wonderful people who are genuinely naive. There are many people, some who can't read or write or have a limited education. They have a childlike trust in those who lead them. They need honest, compassionate leadership, not leaders who are morally bankrupt. Understanding human nature is a tremendous advantage to Cyber Warriors. Instead of fleecing sheep, you can be instrumental in keeping them from being fleeced.

A WORD OF CAUTION: Unfortunately, information given to *Psychics* is often channeled to planes other than the astrological. Be on the lookout for those requesting personal information—they may have a passport business on the side.

CREATING CELEBRITIES

The press is absolutely marvellous. With tabloid news shows on every channel, there is a chance for everyone to get in his or her fifteen minutes of fame. Package the pizzazz and you've got an instant celebrity, with no talent.

The press is constantly creating celebrities from common people. Do you recall the saga of Amy Fisher and Joey Buttafuoco? Joey was just an adulterer who managed to convince an underage girl that he would marry her if his wife were out of the picture. Amy goes over to Joey's house and shoots his wife. In all honesty, how much talent does it take to seduce a troubled youngster? These common people got a year's worth of publicity from the tabloids...Joey even got to try his hand at acting. Ah, the American dream!

Remember Lorena Bobbitt? Her form of revenge wasn't even original in the annals of wife abuse, but the press must have picked up the story on a slow day. After all that publicity, the world was curious to see if John Wayne Bobbitt was good for anything. John Wayne got a starring role, live and uncut, in *Frankenpenis*. Ah, the American dream! (by the way, if you *must* have this movie, it's listed in the SOURCES section of this book—or you could conduct your own Internet search).

Think about it! If the press can make celebrities out of people like these lowlifes, surely you can make a star out of a somebody! If you have a talent for making people look good, you can make money. Put together a press release for yourself and your cyber business or create a special news story or website featuring your client. Make your client a star in his/her own neighborhood. Everyone wants to feel special. Think of it as performing a good service while getting promotional pay. You may decide to give grandma the respect and distinction she deserves. Her family will certainly want to buy a hard copy or visit her website. Point out the good deeds that an otherwise overlooked and nondescript person has done. Borrow existing Internet stories to enhance the legend. You'll do more than create their résumé—you'll make them immortal! That should be worth something.

CREATING PSYCHICS

If you believe in fate, use the Internet to source your lucky lottery numbers. There's a lucky site just waiting for you! Tarot cars and daily horoscopes abound. How can you use all this wonderful superstitious nonsense to make money? Set up your own psychic Internet hotline, using a secure credit card server. People will be able to pay for your services immediately with their credit cards, without fear of their card numbers being stolen in the mitts of the snail mail. Most ISPs now have this capability and will show you how to set it up. After you've received payment, answer customers' questions through E-mail, live chat, telephone or by mail. Empathy and common sense are the only requirements a good fortune teller needs. Surely you don't believe that there are thousands of people manning those psychic hotlines who are gifted with actually psychic ability? Read the fine print and disclaimers contained in any advertisement for supernatural activity.

Psychic services exist strictly for entertainment purposes, if not to fleece the gullible. If you can offer some quality advice, give people some hope and happiness, then you are providing a service of some value. Do not overstep your bounds. You are not a medical professional or a psychologist. Encourage troubled people to get the help they need and wean them off any psychological dependence on you.

FANTASTIC PROFITS

Throughout this entire book, the main emphasis has been on information services. When you utilize the Internet, you are either receiving or supplying information. There is a tremendous need for information of all types, credible or incredible.

In Chapter Three, several Warrior Bytes pointed you in the direction of various information-gathering tools. These are the tools of the Cyber Warrior. Use them to create newsletters and articles that impact on others. People like to be able to prove that they are right and will believe everything that's in print. If you can write a believable story on an alien abduction, a new religion or an amazing animal, people will buy it. They can prove to their friends that they were right all along. After all, it's in print!

You may have some artistic talent or skill using photo-manipulation programs like Photoshop. Think of the fun you can have creating and combining all sorts of photographs to enhance the credibility of your story. Of course everyone knows that "the truth is out there", but people find fabrications so much more interesting. Take a look at the success of publications like *The National Enquirer.* I'm sure the staff at the enquirer are convinced that Photoshop is one of God's ultimate creations. They have definitely been created in God's own image…God is Truth and the Enquirer manipulates the truth, making believers of us all!

Take gullibility to its greatest heights with photo-manipulation. Who wouldn't enjoy a birthday card that pictures their loved one arm-in-arm with Elvis (insert favorite movie star here) or have their own tabloid newspaper article featuring a photo of themselves fighting the most threatening dinosaur? With ingenuity and the Internet, all things are possible.

When you find suitable pictures or articles to work your magic on, make sure that those you use are public domain and not copyrighted material. To be sure, E-mail the author of the website and ask where he obtained his pictures or information. Get permission, if they are his own creations, or ask to purchase them outright.

One writer publishes a short article itemizing a different miracle every month. He doesn't get paid for writing in his local newspaper, but he earns a good income from the little advertisement he includes at the end of the article. He asks people to subscribe to his monthly newsletter and to contribute their own stories of miracles. His workload is cut in half because other people are doing the writing for him. He's even aligned himself with a supplier of talismans and aromatic oils.

Similar newsletters can be sold for a yearly fee to Internet subscribers There are hundreds of successful E-mail newsletters that are published regularly by people just like you. These letters condense information into one convenient package, making it easy for subscribers to read at their leisure. It saves them time and the trouble of sourcing information for themselves.

E-mail newsletters aren't limited to the fictional and the fantastic. There is room for specialization. New ideas for crafts, contacts for overseas house exchanges, exciting travel information, inventions to make life easier, unusual wine recipes, help for specific diseases, etc. If you are interested in researching a subject, no doubt someone else is, too. Advertise your newsletter in appropriate Usenet groups. Be persistent. It'll take awhile to catch on, but if you produce a quality product at regular intervals, word will get out and your subscriptions will increase. As you get more subscribers, consider approaching advertisers who want to target specific markets.

Be unique in your writing, resourceful, innovative and persistent and you'll be a great success.

Warrior Byte

Clever private newspapers and E-Zines (electronic magazines) populate the Internet. *Think Digital* is a computer newspaper:

http://www.trigger.net/~think/digital/

Here is another that specializes in humor and exposé. Author submissions are invited:

http://www.flash.net/~thedoor/

CHAPTER TEN

THE WAGES OF SIN

■ ■ ■ ■ ■ ■ ■

> **Warrior Byte**
>
> *"Nothing is more destructive of respect for the government and the law of the land than passing laws which cannot be enforced."*
>
> *-Albert Einstein*
>
> *Great Thinkers and Visionaries:*
>
> **http://www.lucifer.com/~sasha/thinkers.html**

It's incredible what people try to get away with when nobody is looking. Just like undisciplined children, they are constantly scheming of ways to side-step rules and roadblocks. This doesn't necessarily mean they are born with larceny in them, just the need to flex their muscles against the establishment…to match wits with those who make the rules. Cyber Warriors believe in constitutional freedoms; in *live and let live.*

One of the joys of belonging to the vast Internet community is that the whole world is your playground, but the whole world has the potential of being your business territory as well. Think globally, and in doing so, become aware of the differences as well as the similarities in various countries and cultures. What may be an illegal business practice in one country may be perfectly legitimate in another. If you don't like the laws in your country, set up business elsewhere.

Open a bank account or corporation in a country that is more receptive to your business plan. You don't even have to look after your web business in another country. There are agents who'll answer your E-mail, process your orders and deposit the money directly into your foreign bank account. The era of ridiculous government regulations, unreasonable unions and controls on business is fast coming to an end.

Warrior Byte

Need to find an ISP in an obscure country? Here is a list of all the *Internet Service Providers* in the world:

http://www.cam.org/~intsci/servsite.html

If you need information on foreign offshore banks, monitor this newsgroup where you'll find current advertisements and information concerning offshore banks and business opportunities:

alt.business.offshore.

Many foreign banks are happy to give merchant status to businesses that are new, home-based or located in cyberspace instead of a real-world storefront or mall. This will allow your customers to use the popular credit cards like Visa, Mastercard and American Express. An inquiry at any of the offshore banks will give you the information you need. Stick to established and reputable banks and be aware that, in some countries, anyone is allowed to start a bank. Don't go there—or maybe you should? See Warrior Byte on this page.

Warrior Byte

Have you ever wondered what it would be like to own your own bank? Just think of all the possibilities!

- Look like a big-shot to your friends and business associates.

- Your own bank can hire you for a dollar a year. Instead of drawing a taxable income, enjoy a huge expense account with lots of perks—a company car, fine dining, a penthouse suite with a maid…it's too bad that your bank doesn't pay its employees decently. How does it expect them to pay any tax?

- Write your own credit reports and give yourself a fantastic credit rating.

- Provide anonymous accounts for people who want to be assured of banking privacy.

> **Warrior Byte**
>
> Here are a few more ideas in favor of owning your own bank:
>
> - Provide excellent bank references for yourself, your friends and your clients— you could even charge people for letters of introduction to other banks.
>
> - Issue your own investment certificates and bonds.
>
> - Borrow money from yourself and pay interest to yourself...even write off a bad loan for income tax purposes if you default.
>
> - If you've been really naughty, punish yourself by seizing your own assets before anyone else gets a chance to seize them.
>
> - If your company or business goes bankrupt, your offshore bank can buy your assets for ten cents on the dollar, while you declare a tax loss.
>
> Make this dream a reality:
>
> **http://www.privacytools.com/anbk6.html**

A LITTLE LARCENY

Boy, are some people willing to part with their money when they think they're going to get something for nothing! One of the great Internet selling jobs was done for a program called *Free Surf.* This program promised that anyone could tap into America On-line or Prodigy or one of the other big networks and not pay a cent for their surfing time. The program came with the usual disclaimer "not to be used for illegal purposes", so naturally, everybody wanted it.

Basically, *Free Surf* works like this:

- It creates a fake credit card number that you can use to log onto the on-line service of your choice. You select the credit card of your choice and the bank of your choice, then write down the number and expiry date that the program generates.

- Next, you sign on with the service provider of your choice, using a fake name and address, or using someone-you-hate's name and address. Give out the credit card information that Free Surf made for you.

- Use your on-line account until it gets shut down. The average life is less than a week. Then you generate another fake credit card number...

Right now, you're probably asking yourself "Does the program work? What are the chances of getting caught?" The program works fine. As for the second question, it's far too costly for an on-line service to trace the source of your call. Even if you were to get caught, chances are you'd only get a letter of reprimand from the service provider's lawyer.

There is also a question that you probably never thought to ask: "Why bother using Free Surf at all?"

The reason a service provider can't be bothered tracing you is because you've probably used less than $20 in resources for the week you got away with stealing from their service. Most service providers give away ten free hours of trial time anyway. You could probably surf their site legitimately for an infinite amount of time, for as much trouble as it takes to do it illegally. However, people love the idea of getting away with something, so they readily pay $20 for the Free Surf program. For those of you who just have to have it, there's an address in the SOURCES section of this book. With a little ingenuity, Free Surf could probably have many practical applications, none of which will be discussed here.

Now that we've established that people like to think they're sly like foxes, let's see how you can capitalize on it.

Some websites cater to a specific crowd. For example, how about those poor, overworked university students? It's tough to have to support a sick mother, hold down two jobs and try to make it through medical school. There must be some way to help them out.

Warrior Byte

Desperate students can get help at *The Evil House of Cheat*:

http://www.cheathouse.com/

PaperSure—Term Paper Research Center:

http://www.papershack.com/

Links to all sorts of term paper writers at:

http://www.elee.calpoly.edu/~ercarlso/papers.htm

> **Warrior Byte**
>
> *The Cheat Factory* encourages your participation:
>
> **http://cheatfactory.hypermart.net**
>
> and so does *Cheater.com:*
>
> **http//www.cheater.com/**
>
> If you really need these services, there are more on the World Wide Web. Do a little snooping.

Would you put your life in the hands of a surgeon who used a cheat service to get his medical degree? How would you ever know? A teacher with good search skills could really find out if a term paper has already been used or is published on the Internet. Unfortunately, it's time-consuming to do Internet searches. Employ a teaching assistant to help out.

What about all those contests that are offered over the Net? Are they legitimate or are they rigged? How would you find out? Could you set one up using a foreign service provider?

> **Warrior Byte**
>
> For those of you who believe in free lunches and money-for-nothing, here are some links to contests on the web:
>
> **http://www.volition.com/prize.html**
>
> **http://www.nerdworld.com/nw904.html**

Before you rush out to create your own great Internet scam, be forewarned. The Internet polices itself and you will be caught eventually. You may get away with fleecing a few people, but it won't be very long before you are either shut down or someone posts a warning to every search engine, causing them to de-list you. Newsgroups will gossip about you and people will flame you. Your revenues will continue to drop and you run the risk of being stalked by an irate cyber citizen. Be aware of what's on the web and protect yourself. If you intend to set up a site, be aware that you must give value in return for any cash received. Why pride yourself on using your ingenuity to set up a scam when you can utilize your superior intellect for the common good and reap greater rewards?

Warrior Byte

Here's a list of some of the best lottery sites on the web:

http://www.davesite.com/internet/lottos.shtml

Don't stop if you're on a roll!:

http://www.execpc.com/~datasol/

Find out if you're a lotto millionaire:

http://www.lottolink.com/

There are countless lottos for charity. Do a search and see what you can find.

http://www.interlotto.li/

GAMBLING

Oh, the thrill of winning! The intermittent reinforcement while your bankroll is slowly being depleted! People just love to gamble! Like rats in Skinner's boxes, they keep pressing buttons, believing all the while that some reward will be theirs at some point—very soon. They can almost taste it! The human race thrives on hope and dreams. Catering to this human frailty can make you a fortune.

You don't have to stray from your own home to go astray. There are many ways to risk your money. Internet sites are set up so that you can wager and win legally (even if you live in a place where gambling is illegal, there is no way for governments to control bets made in cyberspace). Set up an offshore bank account thousands of miles away from your place of residence and have your winnings deposited directly. No government can stop anyone who's determined to spend his or her own money.

Warrior Byte

Right from Santo Domingo in the Dominican Republic to the comfort of your own home, *Las Vegas Sports Book International* is licensed, bonded and insured for your betting pleasure:

http://search.worldgaming.net/

Some of the biggest betting sites are located off-shore. There are smaller gaming sites that attract penny gamblers, so you don't have to be a big-time operator to make gambling work for you. You just have to create an addictive little game that challenges people. Games entice gamblers into wanting to prove their superiority over the computer they're betting against. Gamblers have to win at least once in awhile, so they won't give up. Remember that human beings live on hope and dreams so the game mustn't become hopeless for them.

Warrior Byte

Psst! Hey, Buddy! You looking for some action? All the gambling you could ask for, right on the Internet. Just take your pennies over to:

http://www.bettorsworld.com/

(This site is secret so you might have to hit ENTER a second time to get there.)

Another hot spot:

http://www.vegas-casinos.com/links2.html

The Millionaire's Club:

http://www.lucky-chance.com/elucky1.htm

and

http://www.gamblingtimes.com/

Want more action? Do a search for Internet Gambling sites.

How can you set up your own gaming site? First of all, choose a country where gambling is legal. Investigate the various service providers in that country—find out how long they've been in business and how reliable the service is by randomly contacting people and businesses that have web pages already set up with the provider. Next, investigate the various banks in that country. Will they let you set up a merchant account? Will they issue you a credit card so that you can access your money at any time? Will they guarantee that all transactions are completely private and refuse to disclose account information to any person or government? The majority of these concerns are discussed in other chapters of this book.

> **Warrior Byte**
>
> Some people have made money by setting up their own little gaming site. Check out *Cyber Arcade* to see an example:
>
> **http://prizes.com/**

If it's that easy, why isn't everyone doing it? Gambling seems to attract a seamy underworld. It attracts people with addictive personalities and no self-control. When a family member loses more money than they can afford to, the rest of the family suffers. Not everyone wants to be responsible for taking food from the mouths of babies.

PSEUDO-SEX FOR SALE

Who's making the BIG money on the Internet? People who sell nudie pictures, that's who. Pornography has been the greatest contributing factor to the rapid growth of the Internet. The development of various Internet offshoot technologies relating to the pornography industry has progressed at lightning speed—from digital cameras, digital cash, video conferencing, to virtual chat and private websites—all the direct result of people wanting to see forbidden things and willing to pay money for it. Bigger monitors? Yes, please... big... bigger...biggest! Up close and in your face! 'They' say that bigger is better and most of us would like an extra two inches where it counts. The Internet mirrors our desires in every way.

The average voyeur will spend four times as much money for fifteen minutes of cyber sex than he would on a living, breathing call girl. How do we know this is true? Just check the rates being charged, by the minute, for exclusive "interviews" with these special ladies. Absolutely amazing!

The majority of cyberporn consumers are male, but there is a tremendous business opportunity lying dormant for the resourceful producer and procurer of women's pornography on the Net.

> **Warrior Byte**
>
> Many Internet Service Providers ban and censor certain newsgroups that a family-oriented clientele may find offensive. If your ISP is one of them and you would like to access newsgroups that are unavailable without an additional Internet connection, you can source every newsgroup in existence through this service:
>
> **http://www.hotspots.w1.com/newshelp/index. html**

WHAT'S THE DIFFERENCE?

We are all hormonally-driven by nature. Males require visual stimulation to activate their procreative forces; females, on the other hand, are led by their nurturing and nest-building instincts. Men are motivated to sow their seeds, thereby propagating the planet; many women, on the other hand, seek a secure provider for their family nest (this same scenario holds true with many animals and birds to the benefit of the species).

The human animal exhibits differences in gender motivation through its spending habits, as demonstrated, specifically, on the Internet. Men tend to spend more on entertainment and self-gratification than women on the Net and otherwise. Currently fewer women are wired to the Net, so their demographic spending habits are virtually undocumented.

Men continue to have more disposable income than women and women generally spend money on their families before they spend it on themselves. Statistics reflect this on the Internet. Although this is a determining factor in the realm of Internet economics, the fact is that there is *virtually* nothing of interest to the female voyeur on the Net may be a contributing factor.

How does this translate into making money from cyber sex? Recognize that the current market is almost entirely male. (There are lucrative markets for "alternative" sex of various kinds, but the lawmakers in most countries are doing their utmost to shrink these markets—I'll try not to make a comment here about cultural hemorrhoids). Regardless of the amount of male pornography being "flogged" on the Net, the saturation point is very far away. There is still a tremendous amount of money to be made targeting this market.

If, however, you prefer to embark on a new and invigorating journey into the female sexual psyche, you'll need to do your research and discover that women want pornography they can relate to and are willing to pay for it.

Recent studies have shown that women's fantasies are much more complex than men's—more sensual and ethereal. There are several new (and very successful) producers of women's pornography on film, but they are women. There is a theory that only women are capable of producing women's pornography. If you are a confident male cyber warrior, you may want to prove that theory wrong.

THE NITTY GRITTY

> **Warrior Byte**
>
> *No Kids Allowed:*
>
> **http://www.nokids.org/**

There's a lot of competition in the cyber sex business, but the market is large enough to feed more. As in the creation of any type of website, always remember to present something unique and of better quality than your competitors. There are literally thousands of men and women paying their way through university or supporting an invalid mother by selling pictures and videos of friends, acquaintances and loved ones (or of themselves). If it is your nature, these items may be purchased reasonably without copyright infringement.

Some innovative entrepreneurs have set up interactive whorehouses where the women are all things to all men (and nothing like your mother or sister). Others are making money selling fantasy letters or time on fantasy chat lines in private chat rooms. Whether you are male, female or something in between, you don't need a lot of talent to say "Oh, baby, Oh, baby!"

If you plan to earn a living through your website, don't do it in your backyard for the following reasons:

1. You don't want your mom to know that you're selling pornographic... er... artistic pictures over the Internet.

2. You don't want your family and friends to know that you're selling artistic pictures over the Internet.

3. You don't want your neighbors, employers or employees to know that you're selling artistic pictures over the Internet.

4. You don't want the police department and the tax department to know that you're selling artistic pictures over the Internet.

> **Warrior Byte**
>
> Here is a way to make money from your adult site while protecting it from access by minors:
>
> **http://www.adultcheck.com/cgi-bin/ apply.cgi?20698**

To ensure discretion (and your success), find an offshore Internet provider and run your site much the same way you would run a gambling site. It's not difficult and all the information you need to get started is in this book. It's up to you to do the research.

CYBER GOSSIP

While the majority of purchasers of pornography are male, you'll find that women will pay anything for good gossip. Ponder the success (as I'm sure you have many times) of supermarket tabloids! Statistics show that women do the majority of the grocery shopping in most households and those scandal sheets are right by the checkout, waiting to be devoured by bored customers who are waiting in line. The tabloids are providing a real service, stimulating interest and alleviating boredom. Just think—we'd never have discovered that Elvis is still alive without them. Now *that's* value!

Gossip appeals to a woman's need to feel secure about her nest by comparing it with the nests of others. It gives her comfort to know that other people are facing the same problems as she is (or worse). Women feel connected to a larger human family and need to know... who's getting married? ...who's getting divorced? ...who is dating whom? ...who is pregnant?

There are gossip items in tabloids that you would never suspect had anything to do with family. Who got a face lift? ...breast augmentation? Why would women be so concerned about that kind of gossip? I have a theory that these types of juicy tidbits have an indirect affect on a woman's nest-building instinct. It's a competitive sexual world out there. Women are interested in any advantage that a rival might use to threaten the family nest. They are concerned with make-up techniques, hair styles and diets in order to be attractive to their mates and, consequently, preserve the sanctity of the nest. A celebrity's diet will sell a tabloid faster than just a plain old diet.

How can you make money from gossip? Create a star-studded gossip page of your own on the Internet. Offer to send out a monthly or weekly E-mail newsletter to subscribers or to all those lonely people who don't have Internet access. Bridge the gap between those who have net access and those who don't by sending a personalized letter to shut-ins that contains exciting gossip. It will give them something to talk about in their otherwise dreary lives.

There are millions of people who can't wait for their weekly medicine show—their daily fix of Soap Opera. Consider specializing in the personal lives of the stars of one of the more popular current shows and you'll build a loyal, long-standing audience.

Where do you get all these juicy stories and rumors? By monitoring all the celebrity newsgroups you can. There are newsgroups and mailing lists for just about every television show in existence. Be careful what you say. Establish a legitimate source for your story, so that you won't be liable for libel. Remember that a good chunk of National Enquirer's expense budget is earmarked to fight libel suits on an ongoing basis, so keep it interesting, but be able to back it up!

> **Warrior Byte**
>
> How can you find out what's happening in the lives of the rich and famous? There are gossip sites that charge and gossip sites that are free. Anyway, there's a whole lot of gossip going on. Search for *Celebrity Gossip:*
>
> **http://www.celebz.com/**

> **Warrior Byte**
>
> Share some gossip with *Capital Connections:*
>
> **http://www.feldcapconn.com/**
>
> Some fun and outrageous newsgroups to monitor are:
>
> **alt.showbiz.gossip**
>
> **alt.gossip alt.gossip.celebrities**
>
> **alt.gossip.royalty**
>
> and
>
> **alt.fan.(name your celebrity)**

KIDS IN (CYBER) SPACE

> **Warrior Weapon**
>
> See CHAPTER ONE—*Impact of the Internet* (pages 11 through 16).

There are two opposing schools of thought with regard to censorship. Either everything should be open, available and discussed, or everything should be hidden, inaccessible and controlled.

Of course, there are many diverse views between these two positions. However, with the advent of the Internet, the two extremes are forced, brutally and abruptly, to meet face to face. The Internet is an open buffet of information—laid out for everyone to sample, whatever their taste; dishes bold and delicate, too bland for some, too spicy for others. It's all at our fingertips... *all of it*. And that's terrifying for conscientious parents everywhere.

Young, vital human beings have a natural curiosity about everything around them—their own bodies, other people's bodies, other people's ideas about anything the human mind can conceive. It seems a shame to want to curtail that curiosity, but the cold, hard facts are: There is too much information out there and a great deal of it is inappropriate. As a parent and as an individual, it is up to you to determine what information and how much of it you are comfortable with.

Children have access to information to an unprecedented degree. Anyone who has read Alvin Toffler's *Future Shock* will understand that, even as adults, we can't possibly assimilate a minute fraction of this information. Individually and as a collective culture, we are saturated to the point of critical mass—we are stressed to the point that all our natural rhythms and patterns are completely disrupted. Whatever your views on what is acceptable to you, whatever your moral code, be true to yourself, stand by your ideals and guide your children accordingly.

Only you can properly judge when your children are ready to discuss a particular issue. At that time, be prepared to discuss the topic openly. Explain your point of view and keep an open mind. If you have been proactive in your approach to parenting, you won't have to worry when your children come across websites that exploit animals, children, women, etc. If they have had the freedom to approach these issues and talk openly with you about them, they will be able to make informed decisions themselves about what is appropriate. Arm them with the facts regarding the exploitation of women and children in the pornography industry, for example. Teach them *how* to think, not *what* to think and your worries will diminish a thousand fold.

Moral human beings have to develop a conscience and learn to censor themselves. If your children never learn to make their own value judgements because they've depended on you to censor their viewing, how will they know what is right and wrong when they are confronted by a cold, hard dose of reality? In the case of pornography, how will children ever realize that the models have feelings and emotions, just like themselves, if they've only taken forbidden glances at the pictures and never contemplated the human aspect of what's really going on?

The only time ideas are dangerous is when they are forced on children who are too young to make any value judgements for themselves. Witness children who are raised with the religious philosophies of any extreme doctrine. If you sincerely wanted to produce intelligent, free-thinking children, you'd examine every different philosophy with them in their early years and, once they matured, they would be able to make an informed decision themselves as to their personal beliefs. They would then embrace a belief system that was custom-fit and comfortable for them, not one that was force-fed to them by overzealous adults whose "truth" is taken for granted as being "the only truth".

Be cognizant of other people's ideas—assimilate what is comfortable for you and your children will learn to do the same. Discuss ideas in an open forum with your children. In doing so, you will welcome their thoughts as they welcome yours.

Whether you like it or not, an intelligent child is an inquiring child. If you want smart children, you need to give them freedom to explore ideas, even if their value system eventually turns out to be radically different from your own.

Certainly there are supremacists and worse on the Internet. The Internet is a mirror of our global community. Learn about these people, what they stand for, and then challenge them. *We can't change something we are not aware of.* We can fight when we've identified the target. What better opportunity for non-violent confrontation, than to fight a supremacist website with your own website, expressing the opposite philosophy? Warriors who can present rational, logical points of view with simple clarity, will be at a tremendous advantage when expressing their viewpoints to impressionable children (or adults, for that matter).

Arm your children with the ability to question concepts and investigate the accuracy of every statement. Teach them to look for truth and recognize fabrication. Teach them to respect the rights and needs of other living creatures. Fighting back with ideas can save a lot of lives. Expose falsehoods to the bright light of scrutiny. Use the Internet for the betterment of yourself and your family.

How can you make money protecting children on the Net? Look around your own neighborhood. How many families would love to connect to the Internet but are afraid of what their children might see? There are plenty of paranoid parents who want to protect their offspring. Become an expert in the area of safe surfing for children. Recommend child-safe and fun sites. Teach a parent-and-child Internet class at the local school.

Another method of making money is by finding ways to protect parents from their children (at least protect their computer files from an accident). Learn how to limit computer access so that parents have control. Install password protection that restricts who gets to use the computer or programs that shut down the computer after a certain length of time (so that children won't be racking up huge bills for access time). Protect parents' personal files from prying little eyes and accidental deletion. You'll be busy every weekend installing programs and recommending safe chat rooms.

Warrior Byte

There are a number of ways to protect young children from seeing things before they are ready to understand them. Safe surfing for kids:

http://www.athenet.net/kids/product.html

CHAPTER ELEVEN

PROFITING FROM PARANOIA

■ ■ ■ ■ ■ ■ ■

e're always told that "sex sells", but it doesn't sell nearly as well as *fear.* If you think about it, fear is even behind the successful sexually-driven advertising campaigns. The thrust of the message is not *"Look like this and your life will be perfect",* but *"If you don't look like this, he/she will leave you for someone who does."*

Fear sells. It sells books, it sells religion, it sells pharmaceuticals and it sells guns and bombs. Entire industries thrive on the exploitation of insecurity and fear. Governments build mega empires just to protect us from what other people might do to us.

We are a nation of insecure people. We worry about being politically correct, about how we look, smell and sound. Are we good enough... in bed, in the kitchen, in the boardroom? Are we going to be a victim of some crime, some scam, some love affair gone bad, of the monster that is our governing body? We are looking over our shoulders at all times. We can trust no one. Who *really* controls us? You know what? It's scary!

> **Warrior Byte**
>
> The US government, through FinCEN, has taken direct action to take full control over all personal financial transactions. Be very afraid!
>
> **http://www.moneylaundering.com**

How much of this stress is justified? Probably all of it. No matter what you're doing, there's someone out there trying to undo it. Not only do you have to watch out for the other guy, but for God, the devil, Mother, Nature, UFO's and STD's. No matter what you do, someone or something is going to get you.

> **Warrior Byte**
>
> Are you curious about the computer underground? Do not attempt to use any of these files in an illegal manner. All of this is good, wholesome computer security. Nothing wrong with that! *Happy Hacking!*
>
> **http://www.hacked-inhabitants.com/warez**
>
> Are you worried about Year 2000? This site has some amazing free fixes, as well as Virus Simulator programs:
>
> **http://slonet.org/~doren/**
>
> Be sure to test any year 2000 PC fix. Set the system date and time to Dec. 31, 1999 at 11:58 PM. Power off the system and wait a couple of minutes. Turn the system back on and check the date.

INSECURITY AND THE INTERNET

Government officials know that knowledge is power. Keeping the electorate ignorant has always contributed to a sense of security for both the government and the governed. When law and authority are questioned, there's pandemonium, sending Senators rushing to cover up facts, manipulate statistics and propose new legislation to patch any irregularities in the fabric. All through history, those who have questioned authority have been ridiculed, thrown in jail, stoned or burned at the stake. Keep quiet, conform, make everyone happy and life would remain peaceful and uncomplicated. Not any more!

There are no boundaries in cyberspace—at this point in time, it remains virtually ungovernable and unbridled freedom of speech is exhibited on websites everywhere. The Internet is a huge, wide-open arena, undoubtedly the largest soapbox ever in existence. Now, people everywhere have a chance to openly discuss what was only kept in closets and under beds. They are able to communicate with each other, to share ideas and to realize for the first time that there is a world much larger than their own. Their individual world-view is permanently altered.

At the same time, the Internet provides the perfect opportunity for those who are determined to spread their own "truth", as limited and as warped as some truths can be. Anyone can put up a website explaining the non-existence of the Holocaust, for example, but there are many phenomenal web pages that discuss concrete evidence and moving memoirs of survivors of Hitler's horrors. Should one side be censored and not the other?

For the first time in history, it will be next to impossible to completely subjugate the world's people by keeping them ignorant. With this freedom comes a tremendous personal accountability to use this influx of information responsibly. Educators and parents alike will need to become cognizant of truth and be able to separate it from propaganda. This will be no easy task, as we have all been subject to hypnotism by the media for generations and our own concept of truth has been clouded.

It is imperative now, as never before, to educate yourself and your family. Never stop learning. The Net will give you instant access to all the world's knowledge from both sides of every issue. There are websites for pro-choicers, pro-lifers, racists, anti-racists, atheists, religionists, skeptics and believers of everything imaginable.

With interchange of ideas, you will undoubtedly encounter narrow-mindedness and opposition, but with intelligent discourse, perhaps we can learn from each other and realize that we are one family—the human family. Greater tolerance will be the result and some common ground walked on the path to world peace.

Partake in the Internet, one byte at a time. Then sit back and digest what you have learned, assimilate it and, when you're ready, take another byte. You won't be able to eat the whole thing at once, so don't even try. Don't be intimidated by it, don't feel overwhelmed and try to keep your balance. Feed your head, feed your soul, share what you've harvested with others and we will be well on our way to a peaceful, informed society.

ENCRYPTION

Somewhere in your Internet travels, you've probably heard the word *encryption*. An encryption code is a tool that programmers have developed as a direct result of paranoia. People are afraid that someone will hack in (i.e. break and enter) and read their E-mail, or even worse, steal their credit card number. Even though there has never been a documented case of fraud from E-mail interception of a credit card number, we remain paranoid about a new technology that we don't understand. (Notice—credit card fraud usually occurs when the recipient of the credit card number is unscrupulous.)

The US government wanted to make it illegal for programmers to export encryption codes to foreign countries. Perhaps they were just concerned about internal security, but the FBI wanted to be assured that it would have the key to all the codes so that it could read anybody's E-mail, if necessary (maybe it was for their own amusement?) Rest assured, this law has been struck down and we don't have to fear for our own privacy.

On the other hand, the Japanese have a super strong encryption code that their citizens aren't allowed to export. Talk about *Spy versus Spy*. No one needs to worry. If this encryption code is on the Internet, it will be available to everyone, no matter what laws are passed in Japan. As you become more familiar with the Internet, you will see that it is virtually impossible to relegate information to one country. Cyberspace makes it available to everyone.

What all this means is that, if you use an E-mail program that has encryption capabilities, the only person who will be able to read your E-mail is the person to whom you send the key. Your transactions will be secure because encryption codes are almost impossible to break. You don't have to be a genius to use encryption, just paranoid. The E-mail program will do the necessary decoding for you.

Warrior Byte

Win $1,000,000 if you can break this privacy code:

http://www.ultimateprivacy.com

For a free test to see if your browser is secretly giving out your E-mail address to all sites you visit:

http://www.browsercheck.com/

HOW THE GOVERNMENT CAN PROTECT US FROM OURSELVES

Warrior Byte

Spy vs Spy

Your government actually believes that it can save the country by reading everyone's mail. Find out how the FBI is planning to establish a worldwide tapping system:

http://www.privacy.org/pi/activities/tapping

Citizens will be forced to fight back using *Ultimate Anonymity* to protect their system from prying eyes:

http://207.240.104.21/a/Anonymity/

You must be a little bit paranoid yourself, or you wouldn't have read this far in the chapter. Of course the government wants to keep its citizens in line. We are its most precious, moneymaking resource. Sidestepping the norm shakes up the power structure.

Here's what the government could do to restrict our Internet access:

- Whoever controls the phone lines, controls the Internet service. Service providers who refuse to censor the pages of their users could be subject to fines or shutdowns. Of course, this is the same as trying to tell the telephone company that they can be shut down if any of their users say something offensive about the government.

- The government could make it too expensive for individuals to have Internet access or publish web pages unless it is through a government-controlled network. Could this happen? As we speak, your local politician is racking his little brain trying to figure out the best way to tax the Internet.

- The Internet was originally conceived to allow communication between military, scientific, government and corporate bodies. Big mainframes communicated with other big mainframes and, if one of them happened to be knocked out by a tragic nuclear accident, another would pick up the slack. The original Internet structure was paid for by tax dollars and, therefore, should be the property of every taxpayer. Wouldn't it be simpler for the government to control the system if it reverted to its original use?

- Your government wants to make the Internet accessible for millions of citizens. The cost of computers could be drastically reduced if all computers were just a shell connected to a government-controlled network. Is WEB TV the precursor?

- There is already software on the market that can track every website you've visited and monitor every E-mail you've sent. Imagine how this could be used to keep tabs on your activities.

- Currently, citizens enjoy the Internet because it allows them to freely discuss ideas and access controversial material. The Internet could just as easily be used to exert strict controls on the citizens of the world through extremely radical censorship.

Are you paranoid yet?

> **Warrior Byte**
>
> *The Internet Privacy Coalition* has one mission on earth. It is to promote privacy on the Internet through widespread public availability of strong encryption by demanding the relaxation of export controls on cryptography so we can all feel secure:
>
> **http://www.privacy.org/ipc/**

HOW WE CAN PROTECT OURSELVES FROM THE GOVERNMENT

> **Warrior Byte**
>
> What can you get away with when nobody knows your name? Surf all those wicked sites using *The Anonymizer:*
>
> **http://www.anonymizer.com/**

> **Warrior Byte**
>
> For some reason, you just might want to send E-mail without anyone knowing who it's from:
>
> **http://www.replay.com/remailer/index.html**
>
> Post to newsgroups and send your E-mail anonymously:
>
> **http://www.pobox.com**
>
> Try the *List of Reliable E-Mailers* at:
>
> **http://www.findmail.com/listsaver/**
> **cypherpunks/?start=1105**
>
> Find your own. Do a search for *anonymous remailer.*

Modern physics tells us that for every action there is an equal and opposite reaction. Citizens of the free world are standing up for their right to be free-thinking adults. If you are a warrior, you are not alone. Here's how you can help:

• Write to your local politician and remind them that you live in a democratic country that allows freedom of speech, scientific inquiry and ideas.

• Monitor and check every attempt at censorship. Take a strong stand.

• Promote all the positive uses for the Internet. Think of the medical advances that can be made from sharing information worldwide. Think of its social value as corrupt governments are exposed and repressive regimes destroyed. The Internet community has the power to shame those countries that exploit children and treat women like chattel.

- Never forget that Freedom is won by Warriors!

> **Warrior Byte**
>
> If your privacy is important to you and you don't want anyone snooping into your affairs or reading your E-mail, everything you need to know about privacy is here. The FBI, CIA, IRS and a whole host of international agencies can't crack this code:
>
> **http://www.eff.org/pub/Net~info/Tools/ Crypto/PGP/**

HOW TO BE A CYBER DETECTIVE

> **Warrior Byte**
>
> You don't need a character reference to get confidential information. All you need is a valid credit card. *Accurate Data Information Services:*
>
> **http://www.Acc-U-Data.com**

So many paranoid people! There must be a way to profit from all this. People may hire you to protect them from others, or they may want you to get the lowdown on someone else. If you possess the know-how, all you have to figure out is what it's worth to someone else.

If you are a relative novice on the Net, you'll be flabbergasted at what sort of information is out there. Is your lover wanted by the FBI? What kind of credit rating does your neighbor have? Has your boss ever been arrested for drunk driving? Where did that friend who owes you money relocate to?

There are a lot of books on the market that tell you how to set up a detective agency, how to get clients, what to charge and licensing requirements, if you're planning to get into it as a full-time endeavor. If your goal is to make a little extra cash snooping around for your friends, the Internet is a great place to start.

> **Warrior Byte**
>
> Find nearly anything on anyone or any business on the Internet. *The National Cyber Detective Network* helps Internet users get the lowdown. You'll be amazed to what extent this is legally available:
>
> **http://www.worldusa.com/detective/index.html**

As with any resource, there is potential for good and evil. Of course, you want to help your sister get money from the bum who left her with three kids and no food in the house. If you can't squeeze money from him, at least you can make his life miserable by sending a collection agency after him.

> **Warrior Byte**
>
> Track down debtors and deadbeats with the equivalent of your own private investigator:
>
> **http://www.docusearch.com/**

The Internet can help find solutions to many of life's problems, from the simple to the profound.

* What if your mother needs a heart transplant? You'll want to make sure she's in good hands.

* What if your brother is unconscious when he arrives at the hospital? How will the nurses know his blood type?

* What if your friend has AIDS but he can't get the drugs he needs locally? How can you improve his quality of life?

* What if the company you work for demands that all its employees take drug tests and you spent all week with the flu? That codeine cough medicine could get you fired.

* What if your brother, the trucker, can't afford to get another speeding ticket?

When you've got access to the whole world, you've got access to help in any situation.

> **Warrior Byte**
>
> Are some of life's annoying problems giving you insomnia? Try an Internet solution.
>
> How many malpractice suits has your doctor had?:
>
> **http://www.docboard.org**
>
> In the event that you find yourself in an emergency medical situation, perhaps carrying one of these could save your life:
>
> **http://www.am-limited.com**

Now that you're familiar with this valuable information, be morally responsible when using it. Never use this information for illegal purposes or to harass individuals. It will come back to haunt you. Everything comes full circle in life—just as you can gather information on others, others can access information on you. This is truly the age of *Big Brother*.

All the knowledge of the modern world is at your fingertips. Use it wisely. As a Cyber Warrior, you are armed with the tools for destruction or enlightenment.

> **Warrior Byte**
>
> If you need credit reports, criminal record searches or verification of credentials on your employees, *INFORMUS* can get it:
>
> **http://informus.com**

STOPPING HARASSMENT

Warrior Byte

To generate legal threats, insults, curses and flames at the source of the annoyance, download:

http://www.compulink.co.uk/~net-services/spam/

Coalition Against Unsolicited Commercial E-Mail:

http://www.cauce.org

Here is a site that will help you deal with junk mail problems very effectively, without getting yourself into trouble. It also explains where you can get SPAM-free E-mail accounts:

http://www.anti-spam.net/

WishSnoop generates a list of E-mail addresses for people who have visited your website. Find out who is sending annoying or obscene E-mail by using this program:

http://www.wishing.com/

Or try this *shareware* program:

http://www.etn.nl/emailcut.htm

Remember: SPAMMING was discussed on page 26.

Are you absolutely fed up with SPAM? Help is just a mouse click away.

To find out ways to track down the source of SPAM and launch a complaint:

http://kryten.eng.monash.edu.au/gspam.html

If you have an E-mail address, you're probably receiving mail from people you've never heard of before. Is this annoying you? Consider capitalizing on the protection of others from the evil of SPAM, while promoting yourself as an *Ethical Internet Consultant.*

Most people never read the instructions that come with their own software programs. Show others how to set up E-mail filters and give them a general tutorial on SPAM for an hourly rate. People are happy to pay for the kind of knowledge that makes their lives easier. Reading the HELP section does not come easy to many surfers. Take the time and trouble to do it and you'll have some knowledge to sell.

Warrior Byte

The Black List of Internet Advertisers:

http://www.cco.caltech.edu/~cbrown/BL/

It's virtually impossible to stop all SPAM, especially if your E-mail address is on your web page or if you participate in newsgroups. Here's the arsenal for fighting SPAM:

Programs like *FreeAgent, News Express, Newswatcher* and others that allow you to view and post to Usenet groups, also allow you to change the setting of the *Reply To* field where your return E-mail address appears. Leave this field blank or change it so that the SPAM program gets confused. Instead of your return address saying **me@myprovider.com**, change it to **me@KILLSPAMmyprovider.com**. Be sure to amend your signature to warn people to remove the KILLSPAM if they want to E-mail you.

Consider using an anonymous remailer, which will divert your E-mail to another server and then send it for you. It will also forward responses to you so that the spammer doesn't get your real address.

Fight back by checking where the E-mail originated. Telnet to **rs.internic.net** and type: **whois annoying_ spammer.com**, replacing **annoying_spammer.com** with the domain name you want to check. This should give you the real domain name, not the phony one that spammers use. Complain to the **postmaster@real _domain_name.com** and strongly suggest that the offensive spammer's account should be terminated.

Use the filter part of your E-mail program. Set the filter to block all mail coming from the annoying_spammer.com domain or set it to stop mail that contains obnoxious key words in its header like *Income Opportunity* or *MLM*.

Warrior Byte

While you're busy working at preventing SPAM, the other side is working at creating it. Here's a scary site that helps the unscrupulous business person send all sorts of unwanted and unsolicited E-mail:

http://cloaked.com

Don't get angry when you find this site—it's just one of many run by people trying to operate a legitimate Internet business.

SECURE SHOPPING

> **Warrior Byte**
>
> The Internet has its own *Better Business Bureau,* where you can launch complaints against those companies who are ripping you off.
>
> Find out information on a commercial site before you make a purchase at the *NetCheck Commerce Bureau:*
>
> **http://www.netcheck.com/**
>
> Arm yourself with information on Internet fraud by checking the *National Fraud Information Center:*
>
> **http://www.nfic.inter.net/**

Is the Internet a safe place to shop? Your credit card information has about as much chance of getting stolen on the Internet as it does in a restaurant. Deal with an established site that has a secure Internet server.

> **Warrior Byte**
>
> The *PenOp* plug-in lets you sign electronic documents across the Internet:
>
> **http://www.penop.com**
>
> *ApproveIt*, secure electronic handwritten signatures:
>
> **http://www.silanis.com/**

There is a lot of information on the Internet that can help you set up a secure server to accept credit card entries. Many service providers have their own instruction pages to help their customers set up a secure shopping site. You would be providing a necessary service by helping local merchants make their site secure. Shoppers need to feel that their private information is safe before they'll use a credit card.

> **Warrior Byte**
>
> Here is a secure plug-in for credit cards along with a digital signature so your transactions can be fully authenticated:
>
> **http://www.terisa.com**

THEFT

Theft comes in all forms, including the theft of valuable time, when employees use the Internet and E-mail accounts for personal use. How many employers would love to catch those people who are goofing off on company time? Hire yourself out as a small business consultant and set up the software to monitor employee use of the Internet. Your report could be instrumental in determining an employee's career path. There are currently no legal regulations in place to monitor computer usage in the workplace.

> **Warrior Byte**
>
> Monitor employee usage of the Internet by tracking the hot sites they've been visiting. These programs are dead-easy to use, even for an absolute novice. Find out what you can find out at:
>
> **http://www.optimal.com/**
>
> and
>
> **http://www.sequeltech.com/**

There are many ways that employees can disable a business. They can gain access to and alter personal records, alter report data or intercept financial transactions.

Theft of copyrighted materials, like audio and videotapes, can be circumvented through fingerprinting or watermarking, a process that adds "hidden" information to a digital object, allowing tracking or the usage of the marked information without causing any damage. This process is undetectable and very effective.

> **Warrior Byte**
>
> New technology can solve the problems of unauthorized access to data terminals:
>
> **http://www.jasperinc.com/**

> **Warrior Byte**
>
> To learn more about *Fingerprint Technology:*
>
> **http://www.fpusa.com/links.htm**
>
> Learn about digital watermarking at:
>
> **http://ei.cs.vt.edu/~h3004fox/f97/class/dw.html**
>
> and try a program at:
>
> **http://www.bluespike.com/giovanni.html**

The latest crime statistics (available on the Internet, of course) determine that eight computers are stolen every minute of every hour across North America. Is there anything you can do about theft of equipment? The technology is in place.

> **Warrior Byte**
>
> In today's trying times you need an angel watching over your computer. *CyberAngel* is a password-protected program that can track the unauthorized use of your computer and modem. The security center will track the telephone number and location to catch the crooks in the act of using your PC. For more information and a free trial, contact:
>
> **http://sentryinc.com**

What about theft of vehicles, animals or children? On the Internet, there are many web pages and Usenet groups where you can register serial numbers of various items. If these stolen items turn up in any pawnshop and you recognize them by serial number, you could be eligible for a reward. Do a search using the words *serial number registration for item*, replacing *item* with whatever object you wish to register.

If you plan on making money by registering lost children for grieving families, stress the helping aspect of your business. Attack the problem aggressively, utilizing all the tools at your disposal by posting photographs to newsgroups and web pages.

Warrior Byte

Register your missing child at:

http://www.missingkids.com

Don't limit yourself to just one site. Search the Internet and register missing children with every resource, newsgroup, BBS and mailing list out there.

Find a stolen bike or register yours before it's too late:

http://www.telalink.net/cycling/stolen.html

Is your car likely to be stolen?

http://autopedia.com/

Protect yourself, your business and your loved ones with specialized equipment:

http://www.spyzone.com/

THE UBIQUITOUS VIRUS

Warrior Byte

Want to know more about all those cute little bots?

http://botspot.com/main.html

There's always some jerk out to spoil the party and rain on your parade. On the Internet, the next worst thing to government jerks (who want to control everything) are programming jerks who create viruses. Viruses are little terrors created by immature individuals. The Internet idiots who create viruses are trying to prove that they have some intellectual capacity. They don't. Because they can't get any attention in the real world or because they have some other serious psychological problem, they challenge themselves by writing destructive computer code.

People who write viruses are always dancing with the devil because they choose to use their talents to cause harm. A real warrior would try to create a useful computer program. Cyber Warriors create profitable programs that can help others.

Are viruses really a problem or are they just byte bogeymen invented to scare web surfers? Unfortunately, viruses pose a very real danger by causing your computer to do all sorts of mysterious and unpredictable things. Protect yourself! There are new viruses appearing daily.

A good anti-virus program should allow you to get regular updates from an Internet site. You can search the Internet for *anti-virus programs* and you'll probably find a few free ones, however, if your computer is an important business tool or you have some irreplaceable, sentimental data stored in its hard drive, you'd be better off investing in an efficient commercial anti-virus product. Some of the better-known programs allow you to download a trial version from their website. Look for *Norton Antivirus, McAfee VirusScan, Dr. Solomon's Anti-Virus Toolkit, Cheyenne Inoculan, Datawatch Virex, Disinfectant* or *PC-cillan*. Whether you're running a PC or a Macintosh, you need protection.

> **Warrior Byte**
>
> *E-mmunity* automatically scans all E-mail attachments before they get to your computer. It's particularly good for LANs (Local Area Networks) because it requires no maintenance.
>
> **http://www.electric.net**

Viruses come in several forms:

(a) The Standard Virus

Really, there is no standard. Viruses can do comical things, like turn your screen upside down, or they can be downright malicious and erase all your precious files from your hard drive. Either way, you know that you've come down with a virus if your computer isn't doing what it's supposed to.

(b) Macro Viruses

These are powerful word processor viruses that are activated when you open an E-mail attachment or read a document.

(c) Wicked Worms

Worms wiggle their way through a network, all the while propagating more and more worms. Soon your disk drives and memory are all filled up with worthless wormy code.

(d) Bombs

Logic bombs are set to detonate and release their terrible destruction on a specific date—or they can be set to go off when you type an innocuous command or do some ordinary task with your computer.

(e) Bots

These aren't always destructive. They are programmed to perform simple tasks, like any good robot. They can fetch news for you or censor newsgroup postings by erasing them. Some of them can even hold enough of an intelligent conversation to fool the average chat room junkie.

(f) SYN Flooder

This nasty little program sends a plethora of connection requests to a site, forcing it to be cut off.

Warrior Byte

Fight those viruses before they run you down:

http://www.creativeonline.com/virus.htm

Your friends may tell you that you can't get a virus from a reputable server. Wrong! Computer hackers take great pleasure in overcoming the challenges that a Big Name site puts up. They can sneak the tiny virus code into programs that have already been checked and cleaned by the main server.

Warrior Weapon

TXT (text) files and .DOC (document) files contain information that you can read. They are written with a word processor program.

To determine what kind of files you are downloading see *Details* in the Glossary.

You can't get viruses from picture files like .GIF or JPG (so far). and you can't get viruses from ordinary E-mail letters that are .TXT files. Some hackers are sneaking viruses into .DOC files. This used to be a rare occurrence, but now it happens with more frequency. The biggest danger from viruses comes from .EXE (execution) files. These are programs that make your computer perform a specific function, like running a game, word processing or any of the multitude of functions that your computer performs. An Anti-Virus program is the cheapest insurance you'll ever purchase. It will save you an expensive trip to the repair shop, not to mention all the important programs and data you could lose by remaining unprotected.

Learn all you can about viruses. Corporations spend millions of dollars annually to protect their data. You can build a loyal clientele who will appreciate your knowledge and will ask your help to get regular updates. Any small businessman using the Internet can utilize the services of a *Virus Warrior.*

Another very lucrative business is one of data restoration after a virus has caused damage. Is there any help for people who have experienced the worst disaster imaginable—the complete crash of their hard drive? A crash is when your computer stops and refuses to perform at all. This happens because the programs that make the computer run are damaged. How expensive will data recovery be? That will depend on who you take the computer to. There are many data recovery programs available at the same sites that make virus detection programs.

I'm sure you know someone who is a computer klutz (it may even have been you...), who wiped out his whole spreadsheet with a tap on the DELETE key. Maybe the kids played some DOS games and, in the process, accidentally erased some important files. Perhaps your spouse wiped the nearest floppy disk clean as a whistle, preparing to send photos to a friend. Save your marriage by doing an Internet search for a free demo of *Rescue Data Recovery Software.*

There are an assortment of programs on the market to help you recover data, no matter how bad the disaster. Rather than recommend a certain name brand, it would be much more valuable to you to read up on these programs on your own. There are lots of magazines, online and off, that give detailed evaluations of data recovery programs. Decide for yourself which ones best meet your needs. If you can do on-site data recovery, the business community in your city will be grateful and you'll be very popular!

Warrior Byte

If you're still not paranoid after reading all this, then revisit the Warrior Byte sites that were covered in this chapter.

Check out *Privacy Fact Sheets*. Find out what everyone can find out about you:

http://www.privacyrights.org/fs/pub.html

Bacard's Privacy Page gives you links to various information and software sites. These can help you win the war to protect your right to privacy:

**http://www.well.com/user/abacard/
privacy.html**

CHAPTER TWELVE

THE UNDERGROUND ECONOMY

■ ■ ■ ■ ■ ■ ■

The underground economy is alive and well and thriving as a direct result of repressive government laws. If you live in a heavily-taxed country, you will probably see evidence of under-the-table business practices and billing. It is a survival technique the nation's poor are forced to engage in.

It's a *them or us* attitude with many citizens. Take a closer look at what government authorities can do to their citizens in any of the so-called free countries. Be very afraid!

Warrior Byte

People Against Police Abuse of Authority—documents cases of bribes, corruption, torture:

http://burn.ecsd.edu/~mai/NEWS/
police_abuse.html

- Officers can invade your home and confiscate your property without benefit of a trial.

- Officers, acting on a tip about income tax evasion, can get a warrant to inspect your financial records, books and personal property without requiring tangible proof that an offense has been committed. Reasonable and probable grounds are not required for seizure of documents and records.

- Customs officers have wider powers of search and seizure than the police do. No warrant or arrest is required prior to a search being conducted.

- Secret investigations can be carried out by Intelligence Services without your knowledge or consent. Tactics include wire tapping, video surveillance, interception and reading of personal mail.

- *The Charter of Human Rights and Freedoms* or any *Civil Liberties Association* offer virtually no protection to those under investigation.

Warrior Byte

What are you rights in a free country? Read the *Canadian Charter of Rights and Freedoms*

http://insight.mcmaster.ca/org/efc/pages/law/ charter/charter.text.html

- Federal drug legislation allows the government to seize a landlord's house if the renters are involved in any drug trafficking. It doesn't matter whether the landlord was aware of his tenant's activities or not. The landlord loses everything. Unfortunately, many senior citizens have their life's savings tied up in rental property and rely on rental income in lieu of pension. These seniors are vulnerable and completely at the mercy of their tenants in such a situation.

> **Warrior Byte**
>
> "Landlords should be extra cautious to whom they rent their properties," warns federal prosecutor Brian Jones. Just another little technicality, amid many regulations, designed to cause rental property owners nightmares and ulcers while they're trying to earn an honest, decent living.
>
> **http://www.drugtext.nl/**

- The Drug Enforcement Agency, FBI, IRS, Department of Defense, HUD, Postal Service, Customs Service and many other government agencies seize thousands of items and sell them at ridiculously low prices at special government auctions.

- Intelligence agencies have agreements with other organizations, thus enabling them to collect private information on individual citizens. Some of these cooperating agencies include Tax Departments, Customs and Excise, Employment and Immigration, External Affairs and the Post Office.

Warrior Byte

All the Intelligence Agencies in the world are listed here. You can even find employment with them. Intelligence is a rare commodity.

http://intelweb.janes.com/

You may think that this is an effective way to control drug dealers, but consider: many vitamins are restricted and considered illegal! A substance that is perfectly legitimate in one country may be controlled in another. Because of medical monopolies, many senior citizens are denied the right to obtain substances that may improve their quality of life or even extend it. When substances are controlled by the medical monopoly, they become prohibitively expensive, especially when prescriptions are required for their use. Your own grandmother could put herself at risk of having her assets seized, by attempting to obtain medication deemed illegal by the government.

Grain farmers have had possessions seized by authorities for attempting to sell their own grain without using a marketing board. These hardworking family men are vilified for bypassing a bureaucratic monopoly.

The law does not protect your rights and freedoms. It enforces rules that benefit a privileged few.

WHO IS THE CRIMINAL?

There ought to be a law! It's criminal what your government can get away with. Look at some of the cases that have been documented on television and the Internet. Briefly, for the sake of illustration:

- Parents have lost their homes and savings accounts because one of their children has been prosecuted as a drug dealer. In most cases, the child did not even live with the parents and in some cases, the child had been totally alienated from their parents for several years.

Warrior Byte

Citizens Against Legal Abuse provides advice, guidance and support services to victims of legal abuse. Its primary purpose is to expose the fraud and corruption perpetrated by attorneys, judges, politicians, bank and insurance officials and other public service entities:

http://www.ca-la.org/

Citizens Against Lawsuit Abuse provides a different kind of protection:

http://pages.prodigy.com/cala/index.htm

- With the failure of several banks, many people no longer trust the banking system an d choose to keep their savings at home. There are many documented cases of people who have saved, painfully, for years, to pull the money together to buy a new vehicle, for example. When these frugal individuals make a large cash purchase, it is often assumed by the US Internal Revenue Service that they must have obtained their money illegally. Their assets are seized, including their new car, any cash in their possession, personal holdings and, in some cases, even their home. They are forced to live on public assistance. There is no recourse and most lawyers are afraid to question these repressive seizures, knowing full well that, if you annoy the officials conducting these activities, you may be next on their hit list.

- There are other documented cases where officers, breaking and entering a household in the process of doing search and seizures, are confronted by a family pet whose natural instinct is to protect his owner's property. The officers shoot the pet and there is no recourse for the owner.

- Friends and relatives of officers involved in seizures are often the beneficiaries of cheap goods when these items come up for auction. Having inside information about what is available and when it goes on sale can be very lucrative.

- Businesses have had books confiscated on the whim of censorship authorities. What is legal in one state or province is illegal in another. The process is totally erratic and depends on the subjective opinion of the local boards. The costs and time required to file an appeal would bankrupt any small business.

> **Warrior Byte**
>
> Is Canada really a free country? Liberty and intellectual freedom are two of the most essential elements to progress. Find out what books have been banned at Canadian borders by checking *Freedom of Expression Links:*
>
> **http://insight.mcmaster.ca/org/efc/pages/chronicle/**
>
> There is a group of lawyers and legal consultants who have formed a network to offer help with censorship issues, particularly pertaining to the Internet. *Information Liberation League:*
>
> **http://erewhon.mt.cs.cmu.edu/ill/**

- Canadians are facing extremely repressive gun control legislation that may force them to destroy handcrafted works of art rather than be allowed to pass them down freely to the next generation. The political agenda for gun control doesn't allow for any intelligent thought on the subject of armed robbery What criminal would use a $40,000 work of art in a hold-up? Who is the criminal—a law-abiding citizen who is forced to give up an heir-loom weapon... or the government official?

> **Warrior Byte**
>
> Before you vote on any law, it's your duty to get information from all sources. If you only listen to one side, you can't make an informed decision. *National Fire Arms Association* for responsible gun owners:
>
> **http://www.nfa.ca**

During the Dark Ages, church leaders were assured of acquiring prime land for themselves and their buddies by accusing owners of these properties of witchcraft. It was a great money-grab. Citizens of free countries are allowing their leaders to grab property of innocents to fill government coffers, which have been depleted by waste and over-spending. There are many incentives to grab as much property as possible. There is a political will to use money from forfeitures to gain publicity and power. Civic employees are encouraged to make as many property-grabs as possible to gain promotions. Allowing indiscriminate seizure of personal assets is the basis for much abuse and corruption.

No democratic government should have the right to invade your home and confiscate your property without following the principles of due legal process. No government should make the legal process so expensive that victims are forced to surrender property without benefit of legal counsel. No government should intimidate members of the legal profession so that they are afraid to give legal counsel to victims of government seizures. No government should assume that its citizens are guilty before proven innocent, or force its citizens into bankruptcy defending this right. No government should be immune from prosecution and restitution by its citizens for grievous actions; i.e. citizens should not be denied legal remedy in an action against government. When you are facing the total destruction of innocent civilians, you are facing pure evil.

FIGHTING PURE EVIL

Don't become complacent because you think you live under a democratic government. When lawyers are afraid to fight repressive tax seizures or questionable drug seizures because they themselves will be forced to undergo a brutal investigation, you are not living in a free country. When municipal authorities can make tremendous profits by seizing the assets of others to use toward their own pet projects, you're living under an evil empire. Evil disguises itself in many forms. Warriors must be smart enough to recognize it for what it is.

Warrior Byte

Watch out for pure evil. Some forces of pure evil require that followers throw away their brains and not think for themselves. Do words like fanaticism, treason and sedition come to mind?

Here is a group that wants to destroy democracy and set up a theocratic state headed by an absolute ruler, totally annihilating any individual freedoms. They expect people to follow their leader with no questions asked. They have representatives in every state:

http://www.chalcedon.edu/

The Internet keeps an eye on subversive groups by publishing pages like the *Council for National Policy Watcher* page at:

http://www.berkshire.net/~ifas/cnp/

Many newspaper articles are censored by people in high places. The Internet can still expose the tyranny of pure evil. Project Censored also exposed the CFNP in 1994—it was the #2 most under-reported story for that year:

http://www.sonoma.edu/ProjectCensored/

Here's information on special interest groups that lobby for control of tax dollars, new laws and other powers. Prepare to be shocked!

http://www.pafb.af.mil/deomi/ext.htm

Pure evil is what possesses any person or organization to cause physical or psychological pain to any living creature. Some of the monsters are among us, parading as innocent civilians. Warriors must neutralize or eradicate pure evil.

Warrior Byte

A Civil Rights Page for Americans with important links to relevant associations:

http://shell.,idt.net/%7Erpoltk19/civil_rights/home.html

Some excellent freedom resources, collected from around the world, are located right here:

http://burn.ucsd.edu/~mai/Welcome.html

How do you fight pure evil?

- Expose every questionable drug or customs seizure by getting a receipt for all goods confiscated and by presenting the facts to the world. Publicly embarrass the perpetrators or repressive regimes.

- Name all the officials participating in a questionable land grab. If everything is reported factually, it is more difficult to censor you, or use the courts against you, for telling the truth.

- Investigate and expose those who have the most to gain by participating in these drug seizures or customs seizures. Who is going to be promoted? Who will be getting more money for their pet political project?

- Complain to every national and international human rights organization. Ensure that these activities become a political embarrassment.

- Compile a list of laws and human rights that government officials are breaking when they seize the property of innocent citizens. Although officers are above the law when they make property seizures, force them to publicly prove that their victims are guilty beyond a reasonable doubt. Authorities are profiting from these activities and must be made accountable for their actions.

- If you have the time and inclination, use video cameras to document any harassment of civilians. Conduct your own surveillance.

- Expose government waste at all levels. The reason officials are so desperate for money is because they have already squandered what they have extorted from taxpayers. Your country will not remain free or democratic if government waste and corruption continue unchecked.

- Write! Write! Write! Write to newspapers. Write to magazines. Write to television newsmagazines. Your opinion counts. Politicians survive through public opinion and will implement laws that keep their electorate happy, so it is in their best interest to keep voters ignorant. It is your moral obligation to enlighten fellow citizens!

- Get a copy of the eye-opening *Privacy Handbook* and *the Charter of Rights and Freedoms.* Although these are Canadian productions, they contain excellent information that is applicable to any country. To find out where to get these booklets, see SOURCES at the back of this book.

Warrior Byte

Who will listen? Try Canada, which has one of the better Human Rights records. If these agencies won't listen, perhaps they can refer you to someone who will.

The Canadian Free Speech League will provide you with ideas and resources to fight any censorship. It promotes the reporting of prosecution by authorities:

http://www.interlog.com/~mlemire/cfsl/

Canadian Civil Liberties Association:

http://www.ccla.org/

The Privacy Commissioner of Canada:

http://magi.com/~privcan/

As a warrior, it is your duty to expose corruption and evil before it destroys your freedom. Vigilance keeps a country free. There are many insidious forces that are trying to take away the freedom our forefathers fought so hard for us to obtain. Remember that warriors can change laws.

SOLVING THE WORLD'S PROBLEMS

Can you imagine how different things would be if you ran your own city, state, province or country? Do you have any influence whatsoever in the way they are run now? Learning to complain effectively is one of the best methods of getting your concerns across to those who can make tangible changes. Some suggestions:

1. Remember that politicians are very busy people, so make your letter brief and to the point. Address only one issue at a time and hammer your point home.

Let's take the Native Land Claims Issue in Canada as an example: There are many factors that come into play in a larger, more complicated issue. All Canadians, native and non-native alike, immigrated to this country. Crown land belongs to *all* the people of Canada and all Canadians and their ancestors have worked hard to build this Country. Technology, health care, roads, education, etc. that determine the quality of life of all Canadians should be paid for by all Canadians. Commercial operations introduced by European immigrants to Canada, have tremendously benefited the native people and contributed to an improved quality of life.

When communicating with your political representative on this or any other issue, focus on only one factor at a time—in this case, perhaps the discrimination against non-natives who are forced to support native people exempt from Canadian law.

> **Warrior Byte**
>
> Canadians who are ticked off with their politicians can snail mail or E-mail. The addresses are listed here:
>
> **http://reform.ca/misc/mponnet.html**

2. Offer alternative solutions and consider offering your personal assistance with any problem.

If it bothers you, for example, that the leaders of Afghanistan deny women medical attention or education because women are considered worthless, you may want to contact the leader of Afghanistan and offer to work hand-in-hand with the United Nations to have all the women in his country airlifted to countries that appreciate the contribution educated women make to society.

> **Warrior Byte**
>
> If the actions of world leaders are getting to you, don't sit there and stew about it, take action! Here's a comprehensive address directory of rulers and politicians around the world:
>
> **http://www.trytel.com/~aberdeen/**

3. Don't make unfounded accusations or personal attacks. Always remain diplomatic. No one likes to be criticized in a way that leaves them no opportunity for redemption.

For example, the wasteful and suspicious behavior of many senators is of deep concern to many American taxpayers. If the fact that your senator is raising his own salary, hiring his relatives, giving contracts to friends and enjoying kickbacks is bothering you, don't call him a *!~?*@%!!—be sympathetic. Tell him you are sorry that he was forced to resort to such desperate measures to provide for his family. Recognize that he must be in dire straits to take funds from poor, single-income families. You understand that he fears the very real possibility of becoming one of the poor himself.

Warrior Byte

The Internet is a wonderful tool for keeping an eye on politicians. Do a search for *dishonest senators* and you'll be amazed how much research has gone into these websites! American politicians beware—people are watching and tracking your every move. To write to a senator, or even the President of the United States:

http://www.mrsmith.com/

4. Give fair consideration to both sides of an argument. For example: You may have a state or province that wants to leave your country and get special recognition as a country in its own right. It is up to the entire country to vote on whether or not this individual entity should leave.

Are these ideas contentious and confrontational? Perhaps. Thought provoking? Definitely. In order to solve larger problems, it is imperative to look at the issue from all angles—to be able to step back and look at it objectively. One of the greatest advantages of the Internet is that you can tap into information in a keystroke that will give you views from every angle. Especially through Newsgroups, we now have a communication device that will help us come up with solutions to problems that have plagued us for centuries. Take advantage!

Do letter-writing campaigns work? All politicians, even dictators, gauge their current popularity through the comments they receive from their public. A letter is a tangible record of your opinion and can be copied and sent to people and media worldwide. Public scrutiny puts fear in the heart of even the most hardened political despot. *Yes—you can make a difference!*

Can you make money writing letters? Many people would love to express their feelings but don't have the time or skill. If you know how to complain effectively and if you know who to complain to, you can provide a service to others. People are already making money using the power of their writing.

Warrior Byte

How do you write an effective letter of complaint? There's lots of help on the Internet:

http://www.mweb.co.za/consumer/letter.html

Warrior Byte

If you lack the ambition to write your own complaints then try the *Automatic Complaint Generator* at:

**http://www-csag.cs.uiuc.edu/individual/
pakin/complaint**

Don't get mad—get even!

**http://www.sas.shaw.wave.ca/~corleone/
revenge.html**

GOING UNDERGROUND

One of the joys of being connected to the Internet is that you can market anything you produce. What a terrific potential for hobby income! Your hobby will be considered a hobby by the tax department, and yet remain a business as long as your income doesn't exceed your expenses. It's up to you to ensure this, or the tax man will be extending an open palm in your direction.

Take a look at the assortment of goods and services traded over the Internet daily: cameras to candles, handmade Pope Soap on a Rope, used clothes, used comics, useless advice and more! It's one big happy bazaar, where you can buy, sell and get:

- Information (on special recipes, travel tips, music and virtually any subject in the world).

- Skills (like how to build a satellite descrambler or your own whisky still).

- Courses (like how to astral travel).

- Card Printers, Players, Readers (everything from business cards to Tarot cards).

- Homemade Goods (like pickles and candy).

- Practical Goods (like firewood and handmade monogrammed pajamas).

- Live Goods (like flower seeds, peacock eggs and earthworms).

- Dangerous Goods (like handmade knives and bullets).

- Crafty Goods (like Popsicle stick bird houses and doll furniture made from tin cans).

- Exotic Goods (like your name on a star, with a meteorological certificate to prove that it's your star).

- Foreign Goods (like a preserved Martian).

- Unusual Goods (like a Psionic-Rad Materializer Research Unit, which gathers psychic energy from your hands and turns it into usable stuff, like money).

- Talismans (like the Body Guard, a 2" disk etched with a Sanskrit symbol, which will protect you from alien UFO abduction).

- Hard-to-get Goods (like scalped tickets and fenced goods—*Buyers beware!*).

- Pirated Goods (like software, CDs and videos, originating from a maildrop location).

Remember: if you illegally copy items, you could be arrested, sued civilly, or have your computer, video recorder, tape recorder, etc. confiscated. This can ultimately cost more than you would have spent acquiring the goods legitimately. Hopefully, you'll decide to purchase the product and reap the benefits of technical support for software and the option of returning defective items.

> **Warrior Byte**
>
> Want to get even with someone? Report their use of pirated software anonymously:
>
> **http://www.bsa.org**
>
> or try:
>
> **http://www.spa.org/piracy/**

- Escort Services—where businessmen pay a flat fee for introduction to a date. The girls work as independent contractors who make their own arrangements for tips and service.

- Revenge Services—to help you get even, anonymously.

- Repair Services—to repair absolutely anything or everything.These are low-overhead businesses operated out of private homes or garages.

What a diverse variety of hobbies people have! All Cyber Warriors should take up a hobby!

> **Warrior Byte**
>
> One of the many assorted items offered for sale on the Internet—a "Land Claim" on the Planet MARS! *The Martian Consulate,* located in Geneva, Switzerland, maintains a record of all land claims, which will be presented to a legitimate Martian government when one is established.
>
> **http://www.martianconsulate.com/**

THE GOVERNMENT VERSUS THE UNDERGROUND ECONOMY

Barring natural human greed, most people are willing to pay a fair dollar for anything they receive. Most people are intelligent enough to know that if you want your children educated, or your highways built, or your borders defended, you need to put up a few bucks. When the unfortunate situation arises where citizens perceive that the privileged few get more and work less, resentment builds.

Resentment builds when money is squandered on useless projects that benefit few people. Resentment builds when more and more people are hired to accomplish less and less. Resentment builds when taxes increase as services decline. Resentment builds when people perceive that civil servants are over-paid, over-abundant and inefficient.

The Underground Economy exists in rebellion against unfair taxation. It is also a survival technique for small business owners and low-income employees. Small businesses can't afford to hire as many people as they would like because they face an overwhelming and penalizing tax burden with every new employee. They can't simply hire someone and pay them a fair wage. Because of endless government-imposed expenses, most businesses struggle to meet their payroll. They don't live in fantasyland like the government, they live in the real world, with a constant shortage of revenue.

The government, conversely, has a never-ending supply of taxpayers' money to work with. A minimum-wage employee can't afford to feed and house his family. His wage, after all deductions, barely provides a decent standard of living for one person. Once the fat-cat Feds have fed their own pension plans, there is nothing left for the working man to feed his family. Thus the Underground Economy is born.

The elite of our welfare system, namely the bureaucrats who derive their income from public tax dollars, don't go hungry. They receive more perks than the average sweat-of-the-brow worker could imagine, like travel allowances, parking allowances, northern living allowances, holiday pay, vacation time, sick leave, stress leave, coffee breaks, maternity leave, paternity leave, dental care, health care, professional development days and numerous unmentioned and unidentified benefits. No wonder taxes are high. There's a lot of paper-pushing and no one doing any real work. Unless the bureaucrat has had to work his way through school in a menial job, he has no idea what the real world is like for the average worker.

In an ideal world, there would be no need for an Underground Economy and people could conduct business openly. They would be willing to pay a fair share of their income to help the less fortunate and to support necessary government function.

BUSTING THE UNDERGROUND

All governments encourage voluntary compliance with their tax laws. You would be well advised to stay within the law and pay your fair share. As long as you feel that your country is run democratically and your money is used for the betterment of all the citizens, then you will be a happy taxpayer.

If you are fortunate enough to belong to one of those excessive-income-generating professions, wouldn't you want to make the world a better place for all to live? If you love people, you respect their property and human rights. If you are generating an underground income, be a compassionate warrior and share the spoils by paying your fair share of *taxes*.

Your country's tax department has an agenda to enforce its tax laws. It tries to educate people as to their financial obligations, however it also implements a number of unscrupulous methods to keep track of every cent you make. You are expected to:

- Tell the department about all your foreign bank accounts, real estate holdings and any assets of value, just in case they decide to seize them on you.

- Report any safe or safety deposit boxes you own.

- Obey repressive tax laws when enacted.

- Accept penalties against citizens for not telling the tax department everything.

- Provide assistance, meaning your valuable time, when they audit you.

- Comply with tax treaties with other countries so they can snoop through various private bank records.

- Tremble every time they publicize a tax fraud or tax evasion conviction.

- Avoid unauthorized tax havens and tax shelters.

You're either for them or against them! Here is the government's strategy against the Underground Economy:

- They target certain professions for investigation. Those most commonly harassed include salespersons, construction and home renovation businesses, auto repair workers, second-hand dealers, jewellery stores and the hospitality industry (which includes waitresses and waiters).

- They encourage large unionized industries to report and file complaints against any small, non-unionized business that may be collecting the occasional under-the-table fees for work.

- They have signed cooperative agreements between provinces, states and other countries, which will allow them to conduct investigations, do joint audits and investigate personal records and bank accounts.

- They have expanded their staff so that they can audit unincorporated businesses and self-employed individuals.

What will they think of next?

KILLING CASH

How many "think tanks" believe cash might be killed? How many have sent out reports on what might be accomplished by killing cash? Many brilliant minds have proposed establishing a *Cashless Society*. When people have to use cards to conduct transactions, all money can be tracked. The banks will have a record of every deposit and every withdrawal you make. (Banks would absolutely love this because there would be no recourse but to use their facilities. Think of the extra fees they could charge!) Stores will have records of every item you purchase. Anyone who is engaged in an income-generating activity, legal or otherwise, will leave a paper trail. It's a crime-fighter's dream!

You may have noticed that we are moving toward a cashless society already. People would rather carry around a little piece of plastic than all that bulky paper and heavy metal. There are bar codes, debit cards and credit cards everywhere. Have we nearly arrived at the point of *cashlessness*?

Think about it! Your city's building inspector won't be able to receive cash bribes in exchange for his approval of a poorly-designed building. Your senator won't be able to arrange a discreet liaison with a professional woman in another town. Your mayor won't be able to indulge his crack addiction. No one in city hall will be able to go to the racetrack anymore. Do you really think that these people will give up the pleasure of possessing cold, hard cash? As sure as these people need offshore tax havens, they also need dollars. If you want to predict the future of money, watch what your leaders do with it.

Here's what's been proposed as a way to stop the Underground Economy:

- Cash will be monitored through the use of Electronic Data and Electronic Transfer technology. This will allow cash to be taxed.

- No government money will be paid out in the form of checks, which can be cashed. All money coming from the government or going to the government will be handled directly through direct deposit into your bank account. It's already happening. Social Security checks are directly deposited into recipients' accounts. Taxes can be E-filed with money coming directly from your account.

- The government is considering cutting costs by using computer technology for handling money, rather than labor-intensive ways that include minting and printing cash as well as handling checks.

- All cash will be immediately taxed when it is deposited into an account, no matter what the source of income is.

- Cash reserves will be gradually destroyed. It will become illegal to conduct any business transaction without the use of electronic transfer of funds.

- Chartered banks will be required to collect tax on the use of money, thus freeing the government from a lot of paperwork. A cash tax would be imposed whenever money was taken out of the bank in the form of cash.

- Every citizen will be required to carry a debit card. Banks will also benefit in that debit cards are cheaper to produce and don't require sorting, handling and armored vehicles for transportation. Banks will not be allowed to charge a service charge when citizens use their debit cards. This will encourage people to use cards rather than cash. Banks definitely will not do this, however, if there is no money in it for them, so the government will ensure the banks are handsomely compensated for their trouble.

- It is expensive to produce cash. It involves designing coins and bills, hiring trustworthy people and purchasing metal that is worth more than the actual coins it produces. A massive propaganda campaign will be launched to convince taxpayers of the benefits of reduced expenditure if the government converted to electronic money.

- Cash allows anonymity. The government will make the use of cash too expensive.

- The elimination of cash will prevent the physical crimes of embezzlement and robbery. Credit cards will be secure through the use of personal identification, such as photos or fingerprints. Debit cards will be secured through the use of secret Personal Identification Numbers (PIN).

- Currently, merchants are penalized when their customers use a major credit card like VISA or MasterCard. Merchants must pay a commission to the company that issued the card on every purchase, therefore, merchants prefer a cash sale that doesn't impose a loss. Instead, customers will be encouraged to use their bank debit cards because the merchant will be required to give them discount coupons when they do.

- All coin-operated gizmos like washing machines, parking meters, telephones, stamp machines, etc. will be required to accept a debit card. Notice that this is happening with increasing frequency.

- As a cost-effective way of monitoring citizens, cash records will be cross-referenced with other information such as medical records, telephone records and purchasing habits. This will give a picture of your lifestyle and expenditures. Your standard of living must not exceed your electronic income.

The process is slow and insidious, but it is happening, despite the resulting downside of overspending and increased debt loads. Digital money does have its upside, particularly to those who fear being mugged. It has great implications for the Internet, because people will be able to go into virtual shopping malls and make their purchases on-line. Governments love being able to track those purchases. Realistically, with two hundred million people shopping all over the world, it's going to take a whole lot of manpower to track those Internet dollars and government will need to justify the expense.

Are dollars going to be dinosaurs? Are dollars going to be inflated as large as dinosaurs? Who knows? Take control of your own life. Do so with integrity and remind yourself of who the real criminals are.

> **Warrior Byte**
>
> To find out more about the cashless society and alternatives, check this essay:
>
> **http://www.sfasu.edu/finance/FINCASH.HTM**
>
> People survive in spite of governments. For more ideas and information from the Underground Economy, use the word *cashless* in your search engines.

CHAPTER THIRTEEN

KEEPING IT

■ ■ ■ ■ ■ ■ ■

ou've worked hard to generate an income and the hardest part is keeping it out of the hands of the unproductive and the undeserving. You have every legal right to arrange your finances in such a way as to incur the least amount of tax. The big question is *how?*

You might be quite shocked to find out that the money you've earned and the money you've saved is not really yours to do what you want with. Governments worldwide are paranoid about losing control of the proletariat. They exert control in subtle ways, such as forcing every citizen to produce identification when opening a bank account. Statistics are kept on purchases made by the civilian population so that the government can monitor spending habits and determine, arbitrarily, the percentage of tax.

Why would a democratic government want to control its citizens? Possibly because:

- It's not really a democracy. It wants to accumulate information on its citizens to eventually control their movements and the movements of their assets.

- It doesn't trust anyone because the governing members are themselves untrustworthy.

- It wants to make sure that ordinary citizens aren't doing things that are reserved for the political elite.

- It wants to protect the status quo of its privileged members.

> **Warrior Byte**
>
> Try a little Objective Counsel from Switzerland. Here is good general information on Swiss bank accounts and how to protect assets:
>
> **http://www.foolscap.com/objectivecounsel/**

THE CYBER WARRIOR FIGHTS BACK

> **Warrior Byte**
>
> Did you know that in the United States it is illegal for the government to collect any taxes from the people? Federal income tax, as it is sheepishly accepted by the masses, is a blatant violation of the American Constitution and Bill of Rights. The tax code never existed until just prior to World War II and then was adopted as a *temporary emergency measure!* Stop paying US federal income tax legally. Does this sound too good to be true? See how to at:
>
> **http://www.solgroup.com/notax/**

If you are reading this book, you probably live in one of the countries that has an extremely punishing tax system. You have, no doubt, developed a healthy cynicism for any word uttered by a politician and your distrust is probably justified. The reason most countries are taxing citizens heavily is because of government corruption and/or waste. Leaders don't have the knowledge or inclination to bring any sort of fiscal accountability to their office. In fact, things are in such terrible financial disarray that it would be political suicide to impose control now.

You have the warrior mentality if you understand that:

- Any information you volunteer to a government agency will probably be used against you.

- Any taxes you give to your government will probably be wasted.

- Any services you get from your government could probably be obtained cheaper and more efficiently from a private business.

- Any after-tax income is not really yours to spend where and how you wish and you are not free to move your money to another country for investment purposes.

- Any of your accounts and assets can be grabbed by your government and held without explanation until money is extorted from you.

If you entertain any of the above paranoid thoughts, your government is probably one of those in trouble.

> **Warrior Byte**
>
> Need to know the foreign tax laws of any country in the world? Check out:
>
> **http://www.foreignlaw.com**

Furthermore, you probably feel:

- Your politicians are basically corrupt, with money being siphoned off to those in power.

- Your government is desperate for more tax revenues because of gross mismanagement and overspending and must keep as much of it in the country as possible.

- Your country is bankrupt and needs every cent it can get its plundering paws on to keep up the pretense of running smoothly.

- Your government equates power with money. Those in power deserve the money.

- Half-wits, who can't figure out why money is shooting out of their country faster than a Cape Canaveral rocket, run your government.

- All your government departments must report to the Bureau of Perpetual Paper Pushers whose job it is to destroy a rainforest's worth of paper daily in order to accomplish nothing.

Are these thoughts shared by many of the citizens of your country? Would some of these rebellious people consider joining an underground economic revolution?

Have you discussed any of these things with your friends on the Internet?

> **Warrior Byte**
>
> Nevada does not tax corporations and corporate income is not considered personal income, as it is in most other states. Visit this URL for more info:
>
> **http://www.nevcorp.com/**
>
> Or here:
>
> **http://www.corpadvise.com/**
>
> Sue-proof yourself:
>
> **http://www.webworldinc.com/protection/ sueprof.htm**

ALL-OUT WARRIOR

> **Warrior Byte**
>
> Everything you need to know to stay a step ahead of the tax man:
>
> **http://www.privacytools.com/**

You've discovered that we are the enemy—the common, everyday voter who believes the dream and can't see the dirt!

Governments are going to have to change their tactics drastically if they want to survive. If people don't perceive that they are getting value for their dollar, they will quickly move their dollars elsewhere. Weighed down by the anvil of taxation and fully aware of the corruption, graft, waste and abuse by politicians, many citizens are clamoring for a way to fight back.

It's definitely a war—strictly economic guerrilla survival. Us against them. Do you really think that a politician who gets in excess of $60,000 per year, plus perks, expense account, travel allowance, administration allowance, free dental, free medical, discounted meals, furniture, clothing, haircuts, etc. ad nauseum, is really going to care whether your business thrives or your family gets the basic necessities of life? Politicians don't have to live in the real world, with real working people, who struggle under the disheartening tax burden.

The countries that are doing enormously well in today's world are the countries that are allowing their citizens to prosper. They are the ones that implement a flat tax rate—countries that tax their citizens only once. (Unfortunately, Hong Kong may no longer enjoy that privilege under the new rule.) In a flat tax situation, there is no additional income tax, property tax, inheritance tax, school tax, improvement tax, license fees, toll fees, user fees, hidden fees, etc. You've paid for it and you've paid your taxes on it. You're entitled to enjoy it, free and clear.

A flat tax system requires only minimal government bureaucracy and intervention. Fewer civil servants means less waste. No more little department empires, just a lean, fiscally-responsible political machine. Because tax revenues are limited, politicians must be accountable and careful, managing funds like people in the real world do.

It's a beautiful thought, but is there anywhere like it on this planet? Yes! Countries offering fair taxation and privacy in banking are thriving!

Western and European countries that clutch at every dollar, tearing it from the arthritic hands of pensioners and ripping it from the hungry mouths of squealing babies, are now faced with the serious problem of rapidly dwindling cash. Will these corrupt and inefficient governments adopt a responsible and proactive taxation policy? Not in your lifetime.

Warrior Byte

As a warrior, you have two plans of attack. You can openly fight the repressive taxation and banana belt laws... or you can get your money away from the clutches of opulent politicians. Find out more about the laws of your country. Visit the *World Wide Legal Information* site at:

http://www.islandnet.com/~wwlia/wwlia.htm

THE GOOD FIGHT

Warrior Byte

Albert Einstein once said, *"The hardest thing in the world to understand is the income tax."* If you need a little help with US tax law, try:

http://www.irs.ustreas.government/prod/ forms_pubs/findfiles.html

If you're serious about fighting back, try the infamous *Taxbomber's* page:

http://www.privacytools.com/

This book may be controversial, but it doesn't advocate that you do anything illegal. It presents you with alternatives and ideas so that you can make informed decisions. Ask yourself:

- Do you consider the tax system in your country to be fair? Is everyone paying their fair share or are there special privileges for a chosen few?

- Are you paying a flat rate once, or are you paying several different taxes over and over again? Are you paying income tax, an additional tax when you buy something, then tax every year for the privilege of owning something (like a home or a car) and tax again if you want to make improvements to what you own? Are you paying tax all over again when you buy something second-hand that has already been taxed the first time around?

- Are you paying obscure taxes when you buy cigarettes, alcohol or go to a movie? Are you taxed again, more blatantly, when purchasing a license, permit or paying a toll?

- Do your government benefits, such as health care and pension plans, depend on a pyramid scheme that requires the input of many at the bottom to support the smaller population at the top? Does your government depend on an ever-increasing population, through birth and immigration, to gather enough people to support this scheme? Have you ever seen a pyramid scheme that didn't collapse?

> **Warrior Byte**
>
> Are your votes rigged? Quite possibly!
>
> **http://www.networkusa.org/**

- Are you taxed at the same rate as your political representatives? Do you get a tax-free expense account like they do (a special one that excepts you from having your receipts audited)? Do you get the upscale homes, cars, gym privileges, endless free lunches, liquor, office furniture and discounts like your political representatives?

- Is your life as valuable as that of your political representative? If you were both waiting for a heart transplant, who would get the first heart— the one who had been waiting longer, or the one with the most clout? If you needed to go to another country for special medical treatment, would you be paying all expenses out of your own pocket? Would your local politician pay all expenses for the same treatment? Not on your life!

• Do you feel that you need to work three times as hard and as long at a physically exhausting job in order to enjoy a fraction of the quality of life your elected "officials" enjoy? Is a senator's labor immeasurable more valuable to your country than your own labor? Is he/she any more law-abiding than you are? Does he contribute a proportionate amount of time or money to volunteer organizations as you and your family do?

• Do you feel that civil servants enjoy more privileges than you do? Do you get as many holidays, sick days, in-service days, health care, dental care, parking, car allowance, travel allowance, special privileges as those who are *employed* by you? When the dust settles at the end of the day, we've all forgotten who's working for whom! Ask yourself if your politicians have worked their way to the top. Are they devoid of real life experiences that render them devoid of compassion and empathy and remove them from the harsh realities of everyday life?

Now that you've established that there is no equality in democracy because some people are more equal (and deserving?) than others, what can you do about it? How can you protect your *ass*ets from these wastrels?

> **Warrior Byte**
>
> What happens to your money? Who's paying off
> your senator? Find all the sordid and disgusting
> details:
>
> **http://www.crp.org/index.html-ssi**

OFFSHORE

> **Warrior Byte**
>
> *International Company Services* has provided
> incorporation, administrative and management
> services to thousands of companies formed in
> major countries and in most offshore areas
> throughout the world. Information on how to
> obtain second passports and citizenship is also
> furnished:
>
> **http://www.icsl.com**

Great gobs of green are leaving over-taxed countries
and heading for the places where the privacy of citizens
who bank there is fiercely protected. Asset protection
has become big business for small, nondescript countries that never even made it onto a world map before
the age of tax racketeering. Furthermore, these countries
become safer each time a major politician from another
country stores his money there. This decreases the possibility of war and provides disincentive to open up
investigations on bank account holders.

Finally, you must realize that there is no possibility that taxes in your country are going to decrease, except by revolution. Taxes support those in power. Those in power want to stay in power. Those in power want to help their friends, their families and themselves. To do this, they will need a continuous supply of money. That money comes from those who work three times as hard for their dollar as those in power. Those in power use money to buy votes to keep their power. Never trust those in power to look after your best interest.

THE GREAT TAX SCAM

The history of taxes in the United States begins with the revolution of 1776, where the battle cry was *"No taxation without representation!"* At that time, contrary to this cry of freedom, people were being denied their right to trial by jury under British Common Law and were thrown in jail. The British were practicing the *Law of Admiralty,* which stipulated that people were only granted rights if the King allowed.

Unfortunately, today's archaic tax laws are still based on the Law of Admiralty and rights are granted if the judge allows. Many Americans feel that current tax laws, promoting asset seizure without the right to trial, are contrary to the US Constitution, which grants substantive rights to citizens—such rights as life, liberty, property and reputation.

Canadian citizens, for the most part, are unaware that they submit their taxes voluntarily, through filing a *contract* with the Canadian government. Prior to 1913, the Canadian government generated its own income and didn't need to collect taxes. Canadian taxpayers may have been tricked into this tax contract without their knowledge or consent.

Warrior Byte

Interested in some legal history regarding taxation? American citizens can check this site that posts a legal brief presented to the Grand Jury in the State of California circa 1982 in an attempt to correct judicial abuse of people involved in patriot and income tax protest movements:

http://www.geocities.com/CapitolHill/ Senate/3715

There is no law in Canada requiring Canadian citizens to file personal income tax returns or pay personal income tax. All you need to know to lawfully get out from under the income tax burden in Canada:

http://www.nettaxi.com/citizens/DeTax

LEAVING YOUR TAXES BEHIND

Warrior Byte

Thinking of leaving it all behind? Dream on! Here's the lowdown about leaving your homeland:

http://www.crossborder.com/index.html

Unfortunately, you can't leave your taxes behind simply by leaving your country. When politically destitute countries need money, their reach is long. Here are some things to consider:

- If you decide to give up your Canadian residency, you will be required to pay a departure tax.

- If you decide to give up your British residency, you will be required to pay taxes to Great Britain for another three years while relinquishing any of the benefits of residency.

- If you decide you will no longer be a citizen of the United States, the IRS will continue to tax you for another ten years.

The best advice you will receive is to read the Tax Act that pertains to your particular country of residency. Sure it's dull, but there are jewels hidden deep in those verbose pages. Tax laws were designed to be obscure so that individuals would be deterred from the truth regarding the handling of their hard-earned cash.

Another prime piece of advice is to always consult a tax accountant or lawyer in your own country prior to taking a step in any direction. This book provides a minimum of information, but a little bit of knowledge can be dangerous. Arm yourself properly—learn everything you can about this subject before you make your move.

Warrior Byte

Probably one of the best newsletters on privacy and offshore banking is delivered by E-mail only. To receive your own personal free trial subscription, simply send your E-mail address to the following E-mail address:

PrivacyInc@aol.com

All the privacy information you need to know:

http://www.thecodex.com/c_links.html

TRUSTS AND CORPORATIONS

Warrior Byte

Standard Private Trust Ltd. specializes in establishing offshore corporations and trusts in the "no-tax" Turks & Caicos Islands in the Caribbean at:

http://www.standardprivate.com

Atlas Securities Inc. is a full service brokerage firm, also located in the Turks & Caicos Islands, which allows individuals or corporations to trade securities anonymously. In addition, stock market and other capital gains are not taxed at all in the Turks & Caicos Islands.

http://www.atlassecurities.com

See SOURCES for mailing addresses.

There is more information available now than ever before about various ways to hide your money offshore. Be sure you know what you're doing and that the information you have is specific to your country of origin.

One of the methods used to defer taxes is through offshore trusts or corporations. There are advantages and disadvantages to setting up each of these, so do your homework before diving in. Basically, a trust is composed of assets administered by a trustee for a beneficiary. A corporation, on the other hand, is formed to conduct some sort of business. You may be able to use a trust to hold the shares of an offshore company and realize a tax advantage during your lifetime and upon your death.

Some of the advantages of trusts:

1. Eradicating inheritance taxes when you die.

2. Protecting your assets from creditors.

3. Smooth transition of assets to the next generation, without probate.

4. Assets will continue to be administered according to your wishes long after you are gone.

Warrior Byte

Instant Offshore Incorporation—faster than a Big Mac. Have your credit card ready for action:

http://www.travelersgroup.com/
Bahama Services.htp

> **Warrior Byte**
>
> Domestic incorporation for as little as $45:
>
> **http://www.incorporate.com/**
>
> Offshore Trusts have become so popular, they're now part of Multi-Level Marketing programs.
>
> *Prosper International Common Law Trust:*
>
> **http://www.pill.net**
>
> Remember to use your warrior senses when exploring the Internet. Be cautious, be wary and do your research!

For every trust, you need to assign a grantor or settlor to put assets into the trust and you'll need to appoint a trustee to administer and protect those assets. You'll need to name a beneficiary who will eventually receive the benefit of the trust. In the case of an offshore trust, you may also want to appoint a protector to make sure that the trustee acts in the best interests of the beneficiary. Countries, such as the Turks & Caicos Islands and Cayman Islands, that allow perpetual trusts, with no time limit to close them down, are obviously a good choice. Trusts are an effective method of avoiding estate tax.

To help you offset taxes while you are alive, consider forming an offshore company. Here's how it works:

1. Set up a corporation in a tax haven country.
2. Open a bank account in the corporation's name.

3. Open a security trading account with the offshore bank.

4. Let the offshore bank trade your securities for you so that only the bank is doing the transactions. Use only the name of the corporation—never your own name.

5. Handle all of your transactions through your offshore bank and be sure to choose a bank that guarantees confidentiality.

6. Let the corporation hire you as a consultant with a miniscule salary and a colossal expense account.

7. Let the corporation lend you money for whatever reason, preferably a tax-deductible reason.

Warrior Byte

Find out about Offshore Trusts:

http://www.trustlaw.org/

The essence of most offshore companies is to show no income in the country of your residence, if it is a highly-taxed country. Your company must be administered in the country where it is set up, preferably a tax-free country. The capital gains that your company earns are not taxed in your home country.

Consider the following when choosing a country in which to set up your trust or company:

1. How many directors or shareholders are required? Is public disclosure of these members necessary?

2. How quickly can you incorporate and at what cost?

3. Are local directors required and are bearer shares allowed?

4. Are your company accounts required to be audited?

5. What is the annual maintenance fee to keep your company registered and operational?

6. What is the level of financial infrastructure development in your chosen tax haven? Are communication systems and personnel up to snuff?

7. Consider the three C's: Is your contact person at your chosen offshore bank courteous, confidence-inspiring and competent? Is he/she prompt to respond to your inquiries? There is no point in putting your money thousands of miles away if you can't exercise reasonable control over it.

8. Does your chosen offshore center have any tax treaties with your home country?

9. Is tax evasion a crime in the country in which you plan to incorporate? Are the banks obligated to release your records to any foreign body that makes a request?

10. Does your tax haven country receive its main source of income from setting up offshore corporations and trusts? Is it vulnerable to blackmail

from your home country and thus forced to disclosure of private records?

11. Is your tax haven country a stable democracy with fair and familiar laws?

12. Does your tax haven country allow you to take money out as well as put it in? Can you repatriate your money in any major currency, or in the same currency as your deposit?

HIDING ASSETS

How do governments unearth their citizens' assets?

- Your passport tells them whether or not you've been visiting a tax haven like Switzerland, Cayman Islands, The Bahamas, Isle of Man, Netherlands Antilles and other known tax havens.

- They can check telephone and fax records to track frequently-called locations.

- Your credit card statement tells a lot about where you've gone and what you've been up to.

- If the government really wants to find out all about you, they will send agents to sniff through your garbage for any paper documents.

- By examining the mail that comes to your home or business, agents can get the return addresses of all your contacts.

- If you move any sum of money larger than $3,000 (differing amounts in different countries but usually lower than you might expect), your bank will report it to your government.

A smart warrior never leaves a trail. Think before you leave a permanent record of any of your transactions. Keep your business private.

> **Warrior Byte**
>
> *The Freebooter* is a bi-monthly newsletter that offers information on all privacy issues and claims to protect your ass and your assets. Topics covered include: offshore banking, obtaining foreign citizenship, investment opportunities, favoured havens and personal privacy protection. If you don't have access to the Internet, a mailing address is listed in SOURCES at the end of this book.
>
> **http://www.freebooter.com/index.htm**

OFFSHORE CREDIT CARDS

One of the easiest ways to access your money from an offshore account is to use a credit card. Many banks offer this service but there are a few things to consider:

* The card must be from a reputable and easily-recognized company like VISA or MasterCard.

* The card can be in your personal or company name. Your money can be accessed from anywhere in the world using a Personal Identification Number.

- The records of all your transactions and purchases are entirely confidential, with no information given out to any government agency.

- The fees are reasonable, less than $100 per year.

YOUR CHILDREN'S FUTURE

Many governments offer some sort of incentive for parents to save for their children's education. These incentives usually come in the form of Registered Education Plans. Currently, the interest that is accumulated in these plans remains untaxed until the child reaches eighteen. This sounds like a good way to get a head start on a very expensive university education for your children.

Unfortunately, governments seem to change the rules on these education plans annually. If the child chooses not to go to university, any accumulation of interest will be taxed as capital gains when the child decides to spend his education fund. These rules are subject to the whims of those in power.

Use your warrior instincts to scrutinize this situation. You'll have to be pretty cunning to protect your children from the frivolities and vagaries of politicians. To what extent can you actually trust your government to look after the interest of your children? Remember: this is the same government that has decimated your pension fund. Do you think that the political elite will have any qualms about taxing away your children's chance at a decent future? Most governments are facing financial crises due to gross mismanagement and waste. They will always be on the lookout for new sources of revenue to syphon and your kids' college fund will be next!

Many financial experts have estimated that the cost of an average university education, i.e. a Bachelor's Degree, will well exceed $100,000 by the year 2000. Do you really believe that the currently cash-strapped governments will allow parents to save this amount of money without trying to extract every single penny in taxes they possibly can? Realistically, if you expect to be able to save for your children's education, you'll have to keep your money away from the sticky paws of the bureaucrats, a safe haven, far away.

It may already be too late for most of us to expect a reasonable standard of living when we retire. Unless you're a politician yourself and control how much income you'll receive on retirement, you're out of luck. Government pension plans will be unable to meet future financial obligations. Hopefully, you'll be able to use some of the warrior skills gleaned from this book to provide a better future for your children.

THE FINAL WORD

What are you going to do with all the money you expect to be earning? There's a good chance that you'll be turning over more than half of it to your federal tax department (unless, of course, you use your Internet search skills to source offshore banking or tax havens). Start by doing your basic search for key words like *tax haven* or *offshore banking.* Choose a country that's well-known for their friendly banking laws and research their banks and trust companies carefully.

When you do research on a specific country, be sure to check their yellow pages on-line. Most websites for each country have a set of pages that list people with specialized skills whom you may want to contact. Listed among these pages you will find lawyers, real estate agents, bankers, investment brokers—all English-speaking and willing to answer your questions. Most countries also have a Better Business Bureau you can contact to see if there are any complaints against any company you plan to do business with. Some little-known countries you might want to check out are Anguilla, Antigua, Bermuda, Dominica, Nevis and Grenada, but don't discount the more popular areas like the Turks & Caicos Islands, Cayman Islands, Bermuda, Belize, etc. There's a whole world of opportunity out there. Perhaps one of the most exciting ways to utilize the Internet is to help others protect their assets from the parasitic and the political. The potential for income is tremendous as an investment consultant.

In this age of buyer beware, you will want to net-work with people who have had experience doing off-shore investing and who can recommend a particular bank, lawyer or real estate agent. Don't overlook the value of newsgroups, either. Post your questions to any newsgroup that covers the particular country you are interested in. The Internet community is a friendly group, overall, and you will certainly connect with some very helpful people.

This chapter just touches on the concept of forming your own offshore company. It was written simply to provide ideas and tools to inform you in your war against oppressive taxation. Be sure to research the information diligently before committing your cash, but don't let unfamiliar territory scare you. Fortunes have been made by groups of small investors who pooled their money to form an offshore retirement fund or small investing company. You don't have to be a millionaire to investigate the advantages of forming an offshore corporation. Remember, tax laws in tax haven countries are very simple—they don't exist. However, tax laws in taxing countries are usually very complex. Therefore, always speak with a good tax lawyer in your home country to double-check the information you have.

> **Warrior Byte**
>
> You may not trust paper currency—and for good reason. After all, it's only paper. E-gold is backed 100%, gram for gram, by physical gold and may be a way to relocate assets discreetly. Investigate this new way of handling currency:
>
> **http://www.E-Gold.com**

CHAPTER FOURTEEN

POWER SURFING

■ ■ ■ ■ ■ ■ ■

hy do we have belly buttons? Why do birds sing? What is the meaning of life? Our curiosity drives us to understand ourselves and the world around us. The more we know, the smarter we appear to be. Hopefully, after reading this book, you'll not only *appear* smarter, you'll *be* smarter.

The foregoing chapters have guided you through the Net to a wealth of money-making ideas. By now I'm sure you're positively flabbergasted by the potential— and that's just the tip of the iceberg. Neither one book nor a hundred books would be enough to expose the unlimited possibilities there are on the Internet to earn money. Put yourself through your paces—the Internet is so vast, with web pages numbering in the millions, that it's imperative that you develop your own search strategy.

Use this chapter as a test of your Internet skill... your *Net Tutorial.* How good are you at tracking down unusual bits of information and organizing the pieces into usable facts? You'll be surprised at how much you've learned from reading through the previous chapters.

SUPPOSE YOU WERE A MYSTERY WRITER

Let's suppose that you're a mystery writer and you want to check your plot for accuracy. You are writing a typical good vs evil story. Your characters are the sinister Darth Melanoma, pitted against the heroic Clint Valor. You are depending on the Internet for all your research.

Here's your basic plot: Clint Valor must outsmart the dastardly Darth Melanoma. Who do you think has the better chance of winning? Take a look at the characters:

Darth Melanoma is a petty thief who wants to become a famous world-class felon:

- Darth has to figure out how to launder money from his ill-gotten gains.

- Darth decides he wants to build a bomb and gain notoriety as a terrorist.

- Darth plans to hide by changing his identity.

- Darth finally decides that the most effective disguise would be a sex change.

Meanwhile, Clint Valor has no aspirations to fame and glory. He is motivated only by the desire to make the world a safer place. Poor Clint is a government employee who must act within whatever constraints his superiors put on him:

- Clint must try to identify the enemy.

- Clint must anticipate what crime the enemy plans to commit.

- Clint must trace Darth's associates to get a character profile. Only then can he guess that Darth might implement a sex change.

- If Clint does manage to catch Darth, he'd better find the most secure women's prison ever built in order to contain this evil cad.

Who has the more difficult task—Darth or Clint?

YOU DO IT

> **Warrior Weapon**
>
> Remember: there were some people-hunting tips in the Warrior Byte about *Bounty Hunting* on page 92.

Before jumping into the Net, form a clear picture in your mind of the end result. Remember at all times that the computer does not have a mind of its own—it is only an extension of your own mind. Any computer search engine will return exactly what you ask for, so simple one-letter spelling mistakes can give you totally worthless results. Your search may result in a completely inappropriate answer, or one that is too vague to be useful, if you haven't gone into cyber space with a clear head. A true cyber warrior is a visionary and the more crystal-clear your vision, the more satisfying the result. Interpret and apply the data with a creative and open mind.

See if your own searches come up with similar sites to those suggested in the Warrior Bytes. Search strategies for some specific problems will be discussed later.

Warrior Byte

How do you catch a thief or a terrorist? You have to think like they do. Visit the sites they would frequent. Once you know the techniques that the enemy employs, you know what to look for.

Here is an excellent, enlightening web page that contains very interesting how-to information. It includes links to articles about the government, use of our monetary system for surveillance of its citizens and how to protect yourself with digital cash. *The Money Laundromat* specializes in privacy, money laundering and espionage:

http://www.aci.net/kalliste/

Suppose your character wants to build a bomb or poison the President. What methods might he use?

http://www.nfinity.com/~anarky/anarch.htm

http://www.radio4all.org/anarchy/

Where can you get a sex change operation?

http://www.genderweb.org/

Your search may have yielded entirely different answers because the Internet is like a living organism. Old cells die, new ones take their place. *The only constant is change.* Be prepared to follow new avenues if your favorite websites disappear.

CHANGING IDENTITY VIA THE INTERNET

Darth may want to legally change his name to Denise or he may choose to adopt an existing identification (he can adopt the identity of anyone, living or deceased). Both methods have advantages and disadvantages. If Darth were really serious about creating a new identity, he would be advised to read one of the many books that specialize in this area. Of course, they can be ordered over the Internet.

There are several basic steps Darth can take to get a completely new identity:

1. If Darth is serious about getting a sex change, he can apply to his nearest Department of Vital statistics after the successful operation. His surgeon will assist him in getting a completely new birth certificate in any name he chooses.

2. Darth could run a psychic scam where he offers to predict a happy future to anyone who sends in ten dollars and their exact time and place of birth. Darth tells his unsuspecting clients that he needs to know as much information as possible about their birth so that he can see how their stars were

aligned in the sky over their newly hatched little heads. Customers can expect a more accurate prediction if they tell Darth their mother's maiden name and birth date as well. This will allow Darth to see how the birth mother affected the planets of her offspring, causing them to believe in fantastic predictions.

3. Darth could resort to the familiar standby method of searching old newspaper archives to find out who died or was born when. When he finds a likely prospect, living or dead, he will note both birth parents' legal names. It's extremely helpful if he knows where and when the person's parents were married. If Darth knew what sort of education his intended personality had, he could apply for transcripts and university records.

Warrior Byte

When Darth reads the news on-line, he'll find interactive, multi-layered presentations that he could never acquire from newsprint. He'll also get the latest stock quotes, weather, and in-depth coverage of worldwide politics. Here's where to find the latest news on-line:

All US newspapers on-line:

http://garnet1.acnss.fsu.edu/~phensel/news.html

Canadian newspapers on-line:

http://www.ccomnet.nf.ca/jobs/canadanews.html

Warrior Byte

Some additional on-line news sites are available.

On-line newspapers of the world:
**http://www.booksatoz.com/newspapers/
worldnew.htm**

International newspapers in several languages:
http://www.teleport.com/~links/news.shtml

On-line newspapers in English:
**http://saturno.yadata.com.br/rconline/
papers.htm**

4. With marriage records on his new identity's parents in hand, Darth can do a genealogical search to find out his mother's maiden name and place of birth. He might even purchase a family tree CD-ROM on which he will find millions of birth records, marriage records, death records, land records, census records and more, covering a specified time period. Conveniently, these CDs often provide information on the source and location of the original records.

Warrior Byte

Family Trees on CD-ROM:

**http://www.familytreemaker.com/bio/
bio_3000_lf.html**

> **Warrior Byte**
>
> So many places for Darth to check out! These are just a drop in the bucket:
>
> *The Genealogy Home Page:*
>
> **http://www.genhomepage.com/**
>
> Universities and Libraries often have access to Master Indexes. Here is just one:
>
> *Biography and Genealogy Master Index:*
>
> **http://www.nysl.nysed.government/ genealogy/surnames.htm**

- Darth now has enough information to apply to the Department of Vital Statistics in the area where his new identity was born and obtain a birth certificate. Darth has enough sense to take on the identity of someone who died in a different province or state from where they were born, to avoid the likelihood of computer cross-referencing births and deaths.

- Darth uses a mail drop or remail service to keep his true location and identity secret. He found and purchased a directory of private mail drops by searching the Internet. Darth also uses the blitz method, where he makes several different applications for several different birth records, from several different mail drops. This way, he is assured of at least one identity getting through.

- Once Darth has a birth certificate, he can apply for all sorts of terrific identification, Social Security number and a passport. He realizes that government workers are very busy and only have time to do spot checks on things like *mother's maiden name* and *Commissioner of Oaths*. The odds are good that one of his new identities will become legitimate. He will have a Social Security Number, so that he can work under his new name and he will have a passport so that he can inflict himself on the rest of the world.

METHODS YOUR HERO CAN USE

Warrior Byte

Clint is too self-contained to pay a private investigator hundreds of dollars to find the same information he could obtain himself for a fraction of the cost. Before he hires a stranger, purchases a cheap car or marries his sweetheart, Clint gets the goods first at one of the many Internet resources like this one:

http://www.usatrace.com/

In case Clint needs a little more help, there is protection against bombs and poisons here:

http://www.fightercrime.com/lsafety.htm

Poor Clint isn't done for yet. There are lots of cheap databases he can access to gather the goods on Darth:

- Darth's past—does he have a criminal record?

> **Warrior Byte**
>
> If Darth has committed a felony during his criminal career, a record search will uncover his past:
>
> **http://www.diligence.com/**
>
> Clint doesn't trust his daughter's new boyfriend. To find out if the guy has a criminal record, Clint contacts the Federal Bureau of Prisons:
>
> **http://www.bop.government/**

- Darth's old address—perhaps someone in that neighborhood would know where Darth is heading.

- Darth's relatives—Clint might be able to arrange an interview.

- Credit records—where does Darth like to spend money?

> **Warrior Byte**
>
> *Associated Credit Bureaus* is an international organization with over 1,500 members:
>
> **http://www.acb-credit.com/**

Clint can get some fresh ideas from the Internet that will help him to implement some of the methods that a professional detective would use. If Clint suspects that Darth may be considering a sex change, it makes Darth easier to track because there are very few doctors who perform this unorthodox procedure. Sooner or later, Darth will resurface to wreak havoc again... and Clint can get back on the trail.

UNDERGROUND STRATEGIES

Any search is strictly trial and error. If you've read this book in its entirety, you have all the information you need to unravel the elusive, rare and unusual. Searches often bog down because a person hasn't learned to assemble the information in a useable format. This requires thinking on a broad scale and the development of strong organizational skills. For example, if you only have a person's name and you want to find his location, you'll have to think like a detective. Do you know his last address? Do you know what kind of car he drives and what kind of work he does, if any? Can you locate his friends or family? Does he have any distinguishing characteristics? Does he require medical treatment? There are many Internet sites run by experienced detectives, where you can go for clues.

Warrior Byte

Hints for tracking down missing persons:

http://home.pdg.net/bge/trackstar

and

http://www.pinall.com/nais/

Information comes from many on-line sources. Use the Internet like you would use any library. In fact, you should start your research for a specific subject using an on-line library. You'll be amazed at the information your local library contains. Librarians also have access to private databases that they can search for free or at minimal cost to you. They are trained to do research and can often find answers to the most obscure questions.

> **Warrior Byte**
>
> Let the *Electric Library* help you research your term paper.
>
> **http://www.elibrary.com/**

Don't limit yourself to public libraries. There are other speciality libraries that employ qualified research assistants to help you. Many of them have web pages where you can gather preliminary information before approaching them for in-depth data searches. Consider getting information from:

Legal libraries	Medical libraries
Historical archives	Newspaper archives
Genealogical libraries	Government libraries
Environmental libraries	Technical & trade libraries
Corporate libraries	Privately funded libraries

A lot of information is as close as your telephone. Call up a government office—your local government office is one huge tax-supported database. You paid for it, use it—just pick up the phone and ask them anything. Every city has a listing for a government information line. There are blue pages in most telephone books containing the phone numbers of various government help lines. The employees answering these lines have free access to numerous databases and can point you in the right direction.

When inquiring at any government office, be sure to ask if they have an Internet website. This way, you can access a lot of information anonymously, rather than using the telephone system, where many government offices keep phone log records.

DATABASES ON-LINE

Do a search for *databases* and you'll see that information is available on any subject, person or corporation you can name. There are databases for court transcripts, zoning by-laws, statistics, polls, audits, taxes and more. All of these databases are easily accessed and brimming with information on any subject you can think of.

Here's an example of some of the public information databases:

Credit Bureau Information   Vital Statistics
Personal Property Security   Land Titles
Press Reports   Public Hearings
Professional Licenses   Corporate Ownership
Municipal Bylaws

In addition to databases, CD-ROMS can be purchased that contain huge databases on any particular
subject. For example, many magazines, like TIME, will
sell CDs containing all their past issues, fully indexed
for your convenience. These can be quick reference
tools, especially for significant world events.

If you intend to specialize in one particular area of
research, you would be wise to subscribe to an on-line
search service. Although they cost money, they can save
you a bundle in the long run. Here are a few reasons you
may want to subscribe:

- Your time is valuable. A computer search is fast
  and efficient, rendering it more cost effective.

- Computer databases are current, providing you
  with up-to-the-minute information.

- Many databases are cross-referenced to ensure
  accuracy of information.

- Databases allow you to form conclusions based
  on separate concepts. For example: Two widely
  varying topics like *environmental disaster* and
  political corruption can be examined for common
  links and names, when cross-referenced.

- Computers allow huge amounts of data to be
  stored in one location. This would be impossible
  using paper and print.

- You can conduct your fishing expeditions any
  time, day or night.

- If you are running your own business, the cost for
  searching a database is tax deductible.

> **Warrior Byte**
>
> Here is a database for IT professionals where they can research products and services needed for corporate computing. The site provides product information, independent evaluation and the experience of technical experts. Use of this database is free:
>
> **http://www.dci.com/**

YOU'LL BE VERY SORRY IF...

- You don't bookmark or save the results of your searches.

- You don't check your spelling before conducting an Internet search.

- You rely only on one favorite search engine.

- You don't organize your search resources so you know which engine is most likely to find an answer to your specific inquiry.

- You don't use key words to quantify your query, thereby pointing you to the right database. Some of these quantifiers are *How many,* as in *How many Californians own Toyotas? How much,* as in *How much money did the Queen of England make last year? What kind,* as in *What kind of dog makes the best family pet?*

- You don't use the five W's when sniffing out info. Remember to ask *"Who, what, where, when and why?"*

- You don't take advantage of someone else's expertise. An Internet web page, a cyber mentor, a book, all are invaluable in helping you avoid pitfalls.

Remember: Don't ever be afraid to ask questions—you might learn something.

> **Warrior Byte**
>
> The ERIC database *(Educational Resources Information Center)* is a great place to snoop around. Educators are invited to ask questions and answers will be sent within 48 hours:
>
> **http://ericir.syr.edu/**
>
> Another great database for all your medical information needs is at:
>
> **http://www.MedsiteNavigator.com/**

THE JOY OF SLEUTHING

Searching databases is so simple and fascinating, it's hard to understand why more people don't make the effort. This is your opportunity!

A stealthy Cyber Warrior can compile obscure bits of information from various sources with some sensational results! Newspaper reporters have successfully uncovered major scandals using these techniques, but many only want to use the Internet to read up on local zoning bylaws. When you do peruse the bylaws, you may discover that the mayor's son has an interest in a proposed shopping center for our community! Revelations like this have come to people who simply follow web links. Obscure discoveries will be made more frequently as more data comes on-line.

Don't underestimate the power of knowledge. Civilizations and governments have been influenced and altered drastically by the few people who possessed it!

CHAPTER FIFTEEN

IT'S NOT OVER

■ ■ ■ ■ ■ ■ ■

nowledge by itself is neutral. The application of knowledge (also known as knowledge in action) is not. It is the tool that will carve the destiny of mankind. Used pro-actively, knowledge will raise the consciousness of collective humanity to its ultimate expression. Used for evil purposes, knowledge will be the instrument of destruction of our planet, particle by particle. For every positive there is a negative. It is Universal Law. Apply your knowledge accordingly and use it responsibly.

A little knowledge will always give you the edge in your personal and your business life. You may not agree with everything that's been written in this book, but you should rejoice in the fact that you still have the freedom to access information without censorship and to protest against what you find disagreeable. *Get angry! Get inspired! Get going! Do something!*

We live in a world where superstition and ignorance abound. People would rather pay a charlatan to pray for a cure than support research that will produce one. Usually, when people don't understand something, they tend to create a reality they can identify with and thereby understand, based on their own limited frame of reference. The result is an immovable narrow-mindedness, racial and religious intolerance. Will the Internet provide a solution by presenting enough information to a broad enough audience that maybe someone, somewhere will learn and understand?

The Internet provides the opportunity to reach diverse cultures and religions, advancing communication and understanding among them. Unfortunately, greed is a common denominator among all people, growing, probably, from a primal need to acquire resources for the purpose of survival. Beyond acquisition lies accumulation—a symptom of greed, an offshoot of fear.

Utilize your newfound ability to generate income not for excess, but to elevate the economic position of your family and others in your sphere of influence. Embrace the Internet and its exciting, endless possibilities. Whether you're connected with the most modern technology or with an old 386PC, use your passion to make a profit.

INDEPENDENT LIVING

Access to the Internet is a giant step toward complete, personal independence. Just think—if you were truly independent, you would be completely self-sufficient. You could collect solar energy to run your household, grow your own food, make your own clothes and leave the problems of the world behind. Such a lifestyle takes initiative and a special self-contained personality. Most of us, however, are interdependent; thus, we tolerate the everyday problems imposed upon us by others. We are forced to make a living despite the inevitable breakdowns in equipment, in our families and ourselves.

Realistically, we can all take a few bytes of independence from the Net. For a senior citizen, that may mean simply being able to have groceries delivered to their home, relieving them of stress and worry. For the physically challenged, the Net provides an unparalleled opportunity to work at home—to become self-supporting and independent, increasing their self-worth enormously and allowing them to build a social network. It can become a lifeline to the outside world. For a single mom on social assistance, with small children at her feet, the Internet gives her the opportunity to continue her education and build a bright future for her family.

Perhaps the following concept stems from a naive idealism, but I personally believe that mankind evolves upward. Many countries, with tainted histories in the human rights arena, have brought down their walls and opened up to the world. We are living in an age of miracles, of unprecedented change.

The Internet is the central instrument of change on this planet. As wealthy countries progress technologically, our old computers will need to find homes with the disadvantaged in their home nations. As the disadvantaged are able to upgrade, the old computers can be shipped, rather than to the junk pile, to third world countries. And so the freedom will spread. Third world governments will allow the technology because they will not survive in the global economy without it. It won't be simple, it won't be without incident or obstacle, but it will happen.

TECHNO-PHOBIA

There's a party going on and the whole world's invited! That means you! What's stopping you from jumping into the Net? Here are some of the most popular excuses:

"I've come this far without this newfangled stuff—what do I need it now for?"

Technology is here now—you are here now. Now is all there is.

"I'm not smart enough to figure out all that computer 'technogarble'."

Hey! No one is looking over your shoulder, waiting to crack a ruler over your knuckles if you make a mistake. Learn at your own pace, at any time of the day or night. There are so many newbies on the Net—and they all had to start somewhere.

"I don't want my kids to see pornography. What if they encounter a child molester on the Net?"

You are obviously a conscientious parent. That's great! I'm sure you'll be able to educate them to be Net-smart, just as you've taught them to be street smart. Investigate some of the protective software, for your own peace of mind. Knowing you've given your kids a strong moral foundation, trust and respect their ability to make informed decisions.

"I'm scared that a terrible virus is going to destroy my computer system."

Buy anti-virus protection.

"I'm scared that a member of my family will become so addicted to the Internet that they won't be able to function in the real world."

There are people who can't handle alcohol, recreational drugs, food, sex, cigarettes or relationships. These people have problems and they're going to need help. Don't let their baggage be an excuse for you not enjoying your own life and doing what you want to do.

"I'm afraid that if I set up a new business it will fail."

You'll never know unless you try. Find a subject on the Net that interests you and take one step at a time until you're comfortable enough to take the next step. Don't make any huge financial commitment, just invest a little time and watch you and your business both grow!

"I'm afraid that if I get too successful, I'll be taking on new problems like more taxes and business headaches."

Consider yourself lucky when this happens! Hire experts to help you with the things you aren't familiar with. Don't let ignorance stop you—you'll learn as you go and grow as you learn!

"The Internet will take too much time away from my family."

I know your family is important to you—think of how much your family could benefit from the Net in terms of income and knowledge. Like a television, the Internet is a valuable tool—use it wisely, use discretion and common sense.

You have a lot to contribute to the Cyber World. It's a new and exciting business and you have only yourself to answer to. Remember: There's nothing to fear but fear itself!

WHAT YOU'VE LEARNED

You may not even realize how much you've learned just by reading through this book. At the very least, you've gained an understanding that:

- Those who have access to knowledge and the skills to retrieve it will win the economic war.

- You have to make your own plan of action. Waiting for your government to help you will result in a waste of valuable time and resources. Take control of your own destiny and the future of your family. No government will do that for you.

- You must protect your family, your assets and yourself from a self-serving bureaucracy.

- Business practices that are unacceptable by one government are welcomed openly in other countries.

- The Internet is like a giant, exploding supernova, which is ever-expanding. It changes every second of every day. It's one of the fastest, most cost-effective methods of gathering current and valuable information.

- Like it or not, the Internet won't be censored anytime in the near future. It's the ultimate freedom for the people. If you find a piece of information is missing one day, or if a website is forced down, it will appear somewhere else the next.

- No matter what your age or physical limitation, you can take advantage of this modern technology. Get with it or you'll be left behind!

- You don't have to be a genius or a member of MENSA to use the Internet. If you don't know what MENSA is, you know how to search the Net to find out. Use the Internet and learn what the MENSAS know. Your IQ has just gone up!

- You've learned that this book is only the beginning. Keep learning.

Warrior Bytes have guided you through these pages, to the Net. It's a jungle in there and this book is a map of that jungle. You'll have to get to where you're going on your own. Remember: knowledge is your shield as well as your weapon. Armed with it and a mouse, the Cyber Warrior is ultimately responsible for his own success!

There are no Warrior Bytes in this chapter because it's time to enter the combat zone on your own. You've finished basic training. Should you wish to contact the author, use your newfound Internet skills to find the E-mail address. I welcome your comments and suggestions. If we all share information and ideas, the Internet will become the best research resource ever.

NOW—TAKE A BYTE AND ENJOY!

Glossary

> **Warrior Weapon**
>
> There is a complete glossary on the Internet. See Warrior Byte on page 4 for details.

Browser
In order to see the various web pages on the Internet, you need a computer program which recognizes the HTML computer language. Two common browsers are *Netscape* and *Internet Explorer*. Some ISPs provide their own specific browsers.

BBS
Bulletin Board System—usually accessed through *telnet* and run by hobbyists. They provide a place for people to post and receive information on topics of special interest.

Boot
To start up your computer.

Chat
To communicate with other people in real time using your keyboard.

Cookie
A little piece of information that is saved in your browser for later access. Cookies aren't dangerous. They can't get anything about you that you didn't want to reveal. They usually store preferences, like what web browser you prefer to use and what password you use to get into restricted sites.

Cyber

Computer networking form your home to the world.

Details

When using the WINDOWS EXPLORER, you can click on VIEW then DETAILS in order to see the type of file you may be considering opening. Files that end in .ZIP need a special program to unzip them. Files that end in .TXT or .DOC need a word processor program to view them. Files that end in .JPG or .GIF contain pictures that can be viewed in your web browser. Program files that end in .EXE can often contain viruses if they come from an unknown source. Be sure to get your files from a reputable Internet site.

Domain Name

A snappy way of contacting a specific Internet address. Instead of using a long IP number like 207.102.137.15 you can simply type ISLANDNET into your web browser to arrive at that destination.

DOS

Disk Operating System—makes your computer do practical things for you, like copy disks and move files.

E-Mail

Electronic Mail—faster than the post office and more convenient than putting a telephone in your shower. Cheaper than either the telephone company or post office. E-mail is the number one reason people connect to the Internet. Every ISP carries an E-mail program for its customers.

E-Zine

Electronic Magazine—like magazines published on paper, e-zines are published on a regular basis and have subscribers.

Finger
A utility program that allows you to obtain information about other Internet users who have E-mail accounts.

Flame
To make inflammatory remarks to people by assaulting their character or ideas.

Font
A typographic style for printing. There are thousands of different fonts. Some common ones that your word processor might use are Arial, Times New Roman, and Courier.

FTP
File Transfer Protocol—a program that allows you to transfer your web page files to your ISP. It also lets you download files from various sites directly to your computer.

GIF
Graphics Interchange Format—a file containing a picture.

Hardware
The hard physical parts of your computer system that you can actually see and touch, such as the keyboard, video monitor and mouse.

HTML
Hyper Text Markup Language—this is a simple programming language which allows your web browser to display Internet web pages. Web pages are written in the HTML computer language.

HTTP
Hypertext Transport Protocol—signals your computer that it is looking for a website.

Icon

Cute little pictures that you can click on to make something happen. For example, on some computers you can click on a picture of a mailbox and your E-mail program will open.

IP

Internet Protocol—and address consisting of four sets of numbers, separated by periods. Each IP address is unique and will take you to a different site on the Internet.

IRC

Internet Relay Chat—allows you to exchange conversation with others, in real time, through typing or talking with specialized chat programs. These programs create different channels where you can meet with people all over the world.

ISP

Internet Service Provider—you have to join one of these to get on the World Wide Web. An Internet Service Provider connects to other providers around the world. When you connect to an ISP you are able to bring information from all over the world into your home.

JAVA

A type of programming language that is recognized by web browsers and computer systems. Entire books have been written about all the magnificent things JAVA can do, but most web page authors use it to make information scroll across your screen.

JPG or JPEG

Joint Photographic Experts Group—a type of file that usually contains photographs which can be viewed in your web browser.

LOL
Laughing Out Loud

MIME
Multipurpose Internet Mail Extensions—this allows you to transfer graphics and sound through your E-mail program.

Netiquette
Polite behavior while communicating with others on the Internet, including chat rooms, E-mail, newsgroups and bulletin boards. This usually means no spamming or flaming.

Newsgroup
A place where you can post your thoughts and ideas and receive comments back from other subscribers.

PC
Personal Computer—IBM (International Business Machines) started it all in 1981 by competing with Apple and creating a desktop computer that would run standard software.

PCMCIA
Personal Computer Memory Card International Association—created a standard design for modem card manufacturers.

POP
Post Office Protocol—your POP account allows you to send and receive most types of E-mail and attachments.

Real Time
Immediately, without waiting.

ROTFLMAO
Rolling On The Floor Laughing My Ass Off.

Search Engine

A program which goes through the Internet and brings back pages that have keywords matching the words you type into the search field.

Shareware

Nice people write these programs which allow you to "try before you buy". Shareware is not Freeware. If you find a program that is useful and practical, you should give the author proper credit by paying for the program. By paying, you not only receive technical support and updates, you also support many individuals and fledgling companies that are trying to survive in the business world.

Shouting

Typing your comments in upper case letters, in order to attract attention. It is considered bad netiquette.

Software

Useful programs that make your computer do something. For example, WINDOWS is a software program that has become indispensable to most computer users.

SPAM

Internet junk mail. No SPAM, SPAM and SPAM with my E-mail please.

Telnet

A simple program that provides a bare bones way to get information off the Internet. You can usually access telnet by typing the word "telnet" in the RUN window of your computer, then type in the domain address that you are telnetting to. Many public libraries let you telnet in to their computer system to see what books are available and to reserve books without having to phone.

URL

Uniform Resource Locator—an Internet address that lets your computer find websites. http://www.ibm.com is an example of an URL.

Usenet

A massive collection of newsgroups that anyone connected to the Internet can access using a newsreader program.

Velveeta

Unwanted advertising that spreads itself across newsgroups in much the same way that SPAM annoys E-mail clients.

Wired

Connected to the Internet.

WYSIWYG

What You See Is What You Get—usually refers to fonts and page layout, which appear on the Internet, and on paper, the way they appear on your screen when you design them.

ZIP

Sometimes you'll receive a file that ends with .ZIP. This means that the file has been compressed so that it will be easier to send over the Internet. You need a program like PKUNZIP or WinZip in order to use these files.

Sources of Information

This is a list of non-Internet sources that were mentioned. They are also an alternative form of information contacts for those who haven't connected to the Internet yet.

Chapter Two: Analyzing Yourself
The Foundation for Economic Education
30 South Broadway
Irvington-on-Hudson, New York 10533
Phone: (800) 452-3518, (914) 591-7230
Fax: (914) 591-8910

Chapter Five: Helping Yourself
To find out more about direct mail marketing write to:
Direct Marketing Association
6 East 43rd Street
New York, NY 10017

Here is a company that offers a free brochure on *How To Prepare A Direct Mail Brochure That Sells*. The Information can be applied to Internet marketing. Send a stamped, self-addressed envelope to:
Hugo Dunhill Mailing Lists, Inc.
630 Third Avenue
New York, NY 10017
Phone: (800) 223-6454

Chapter Seven: Imports and Exports
Canadian Intellectual Property Office
Copyright and Industrial Design Branch
Tower #1, 50 Victoria Street
Place du Portage
Hull, Quebec K1A 0C9
Phone: (819) 997-1936

Export-Import Bank of the United States (Eximbank)
811 Vermont Avenue, N.W.
Washington, DC 20571
Phone: (202) 565 3900
Fax: (800) 424-5201

National Customs Brokers and Forwarders Association
1 World Trade Center, Suite 1153
New York, NY 10048
Phone: (212) 432-0050
E-Mail: staff@ncbfaa.org

Manufacturer's Agents National Association
23016 Mill Creek Road
PO Box 3467
Laguna Hills, CA 92653
Phone: (714) 859-4040

Chapter Nine: Money From Writing
King James Bible
John's Story   (John 20:1-2)
Matt's Story   (Matt 28:1-8)
Mark's Story   (Mark 16:1-10)
Luke's Story   (Luke 23:55-56; 24:1-10)

Reverend Peter Popoff
PO Box 1400, Station U
Toronto, Ontario M8Z 9Z9

People United For Christ
PO Box 760
Upland, CA 91785

Frankenpenis
Phone orders can be placed from 9:00 AM to 5:00 PM
Pacific Standard Time. Ask for the mail order department.
Phone: (800)433-3707 or (818) 773-7234

Chapter Ten: The Wages of Sin
Free Surf
Kingsway Publishing International
1 Wilkinson House
Blount Street
Docklands
London, United Kingdom E14 7QG
Fax: (44) (0) 171-739-6596

Chapter Eleven: Profiting From Paranoia
Williams Remail Services
PO Box 835
Adelaide Street
Toronto, Ontario M5C 2K1
Phone: (416) 767-8838

Crossroads Remailing Service
PO Box 87-3892
Panama
Republic of Panama
Phone/Fax: (507) 224-9244

Chapter Twelve: The Underground Economy
Canadian Free Speech League
PO Box 14043
Victoria, British Columbia V8W 3N3
Fax: (604) 479-3294

Privacy Commission of Canada
112 Kent Street
Ottawa, Ontario K1A 1H3
Phone: (800) 267-0441
Fax: (613) 995-1501

Privacy Handbook
B.C. Civil Liberties Association
518 - 119 West Pender Street
Vancouver, British Columbia V6B 1S5

You may order a copy of the *Charter of Rights and Freedoms* from:
The Communications Directorate
Department of the Secretary of State
Ottawa, Ontario K1A 0M5
Phone: (819) 997-0055

To complain about Human Rights abuses write to:
Mary Robinson
UN High Commissioner for Human Rights
Office of the High Commissioner for Human Rights at
    Geneva
Palais des Nations, CH-1211
Geneva, 10, Switzerland

Chapter Thirteen: Keeping It
PRIVACYINC (E-mail newsletter)
Suite 383
37 Store Street
London, United Kingdom WC1 7BS

A full list of US Secured Card Programs may be obtained
for 5$US from:
Bank Holders of America
Phone: 9800) 237-1800

Standard Private Trust Ltd.(Confidentially Providing Offshore Company Formation)
Times Square
PO Box 193, Leeward Highway
Providenciales
Turks & Caicos Islands, British West Indies
Phone: (649) 946-4387
Fax: (649) 946-4928

Atlas Securities Inc.
Times Square
PO Box 193, Leeward Highway
Turks & Caicos Islands, British West Indies
Phone: (649) 941-5835
Fax: (649) 941-5315

The Freebooter
PO Box 494
St. Peter's Port
Guernsey, Channel Islands GY1 6BZ
Phone: (44) 171-223-4295

Index

UPHILL PUBLISHING: SOMETHING FOR EVERYONE

Sell your own home and save $$$thousands in commissions.

Buy stock in blue chip companies withour paying commissions.

Make informed investment decisions.

Financial planning for the Boomer generation.

Estate planning and investment strategies.

Investment strategies from those who know.

Directory of tax havens and discussion of tax saving strategies.

Live tax free happily ever after.

Invest offshore from the comfort of your own home.

Available Fall 1998:

How To Do The Impossible!
Gotcha!!!
Paul & Greg's Excellent Tax Adventure
RRIFs LIFs & Other IFs
Southam Canadian Mutual Fund Guide 1999